1 e4 d5

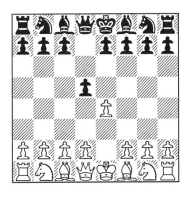

The Scandinavian

CHESS PRESS OPENING GUIDES

Other titles in this series include:

1 901259 05 6	Caro-Kann Advance	Byron Jacobs
1 901259 06 4	Closed Sicilian	Daniel King
1 901259 03 X	Dutch Leningrad	Neil McDonald
1 901259 10 2	French Advance	Tony Kosten
1 901259 01 3	Sicilian Taimanov	James Plaskett
1 901259 08 0	Semi-Slav	Matthew Sadler
1 901259 00 5	Slav	Matthew Sadler
1 901259 09 9	Trompowsky	Joe Gallagher

For further details for Chess Press titles, please write to The Chess Press c/o Cadogan Books plc, 4th Floor, Gloucester Mansions, 140a Shaftesbury Avenue, London WC2H 8HD.

Chess Press Opening Guides

The Scandinavian

John Emms

The Chess Press, Brighton

First published 1997 by The Chess Press, an imprint of First Rank Publishing, 23 Ditchling Rise, Brighton, East Sussex, BN1 4QL, in association with Cadogan Books plc.

Reprinted with corrections 1998

Distributed by Cadogan Books plc, 4th Floor, Gloucester Mansions, 140a Shaftesbury Avenue, London WC2H 8HD

A CIP catalogue record for this book is available from the British Library

ISBN 1 901259 02 1

Author photograph by Claire Smith
Cover design by Ray Shell Design
Printed and bound in Great Britain by Biddles

CONTENTS

1 e4 d5

BIBLIOGRAPHY

Books

Encyclopaedia of Chess Openings vol.B, Sahovski Informator 1984
Batsford Chess Openings 2, Kasparov & Keene (Batsford 1989)
Winning with the Scandinavian, Harman & Taulbut (Batsford 1993)
An Opening Repertoire for the Attacking Player, Keene & Levy (Batsford 1994)
Centre Counter Power Play, Fishbein & Hodges (R&D 1994)
My 60 Memorable Games, Fischer (Faber & Faber 1969)

Periodicals

Informator
ChessBase Magazine
New In Chess Yearbook
British Chess Magazine
Chess Monthly

PREFACE

Over the past decade we have experienced an enormous explosion in the chess information business, caused, in the main, by computerised chess databases and high-tech communications. Top players now cannot make a single move, without anyone and everyone knowing about it the next day. In such a climate preparation at the top level has become easier and yet more difficult at the same time; easier to find out the repertoire of one's opponent, but much more difficult to create novel ideas in well-worn openings. With this in mind many more of today's grandmasters are now keen to study previously neglected openings, and to introduce them into their own armoury.

Until a few years ago the Scandinavian Defence was considered a theoretical backwater. Okay, there were some games of Bent Larsen and later the Australian GM Ian Rogers, but these were the only two top players to utilise the opening on a regular basis, and in any case, both players are renowned for being innovative and experimental in the opening stages. The little theory there was tended to give glossy assessments from White's point of view. The Scandinavian's main advantage lay in the fact that there was so little theory. Deep study by the individual would be rewarded, as the defence was underestimated.

Following the recent eruption of theory, some of the questions of the Scandinavian have been answered, although we should expect many more new ones to crop up. It has become apparent that the Scandinavian has always been a perfectly reasonable defence to 1 e4. Just like all the main defences, the Sicilian, French and 1...e5, it has its pluses and minuses and we shall be discussing these in the introduction and throughout the book. Possibly White players have become complacent, as most of the recent discoveries have been for Black, and this has given Scandinavian players flexibility in choosing variations. Lines such as the Icelandic Gambit (1 e4 d5 2 exd5 ♘f6 3 c4 e6) and 1 e4 d5 2 exd5 ♘d5 3 d4 ♗g4!? have sprouted out of nowhere to enhance Black's options, and these variations fully deserve chapters on their own. As another advert for the Scandinavian one could also point to Anand's employment of the defence at the very highest level in his World Championship match against Kasparov, but perhaps the most revealing statistic is the number of respected grandmasters who have now added the defence to their repertoire: Anand, Glek, Dautov, Smagin, Hodgson, Speelman, Adams, Oll, Stefansson and Curt Hansen are just a few who have attached their name to the list. Apologies to those I've missed out!

In preparing this book I was assisted by a *ChessBase* database program with a *Fritz* analysis module. I would like to thank Bob Wade for supplying me with extra material.

John Emms,
Beckenham,
January 1997

INTRODUCTION

The basic concept of the Scandinavian Defence is fairly simple. With 1...d5 Black immediately opens lines for his pieces, enabling him to develop smoothly. The cost is that after 1 e4 d5 2 exd5 Black has to lose time in restoring the material balance by capturing on d5. There are two ways to achieve this: 2...♛xd5 is the most direct method, after which White can gain time by attacking the black queen; 2...♘f6 is the other way. The latter move can entail more risk as White has ways of holding onto the pawn, although the element of risk does apply to both parties.

I would say that, from the Black point of view at least, 2...♛xd5 lines contain more positional concepts, while 2...♘f6 contains more tactical ones. Before we go head on into the actual theory of this opening, it is important to discuss some of these ideas. I will deal with 2...♛xd5 and 2...♘f6 lines separately, although some of the ideas do overlap.

a) 2...♛xd5

The 'Scandinavian Bishop'
The light-squared bishop is one of Black's major players in the Scandinavian Defence. Released by Black's very first move, this bishop has a flexible choice of squares at f5, g4, and even very occasionally e6.

As Scandinavian theory has developed, it has gradually become apparent that the b1-h7 diagonal is generally the bishop's most the desirable diagonal. From here it often has a significant influence on the queenside. In particular, when White has played the common ♘c3 (to attack the black queen) and followed up with the natural d2-d4, the light-squared bishop is excellently placed on f5. It bears down on White's c2-pawn, which may become quite vulnerable to attack.

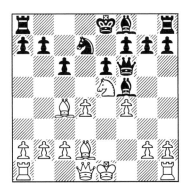

Here the weakness of c2 can be exploited immediately. After 1...♘xe5 2 fxe5 ♛g6! White must lose a pawn, as c2 and g2 are simultaneously attacked.

White often takes measures against Black light-squared bishop on the b1-h7 diagonal. One of White's most direct methods is to harass the bishop with a timely g2-g4 and even h2-h4-h5. Black must beware of certain tricks which either force him to make positional concessions or, in the most extreme cases, part company with the bishop altogether.

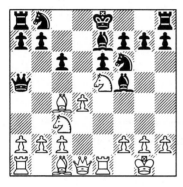

If Black plays the casual 1...0-0 punishment will be swift after 2 g4! ♗g6 3 h4, when the threat of h4-h5 is extremely annoying for Black. The 'normal' remedy of creating a flight square means accepting a massive positional disadvantage after 3...h6 4 ♘xg6 fxg6. Indeed in this particular case White can cash in immediately with 5 ♖xe6, with crushing consequences.

Another idea for White is to delay the advance d2-d4.

see following diagram

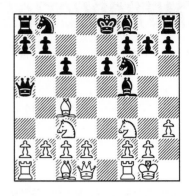

Here White could consider foregoing d2-d4 completely in favour of 1 d3!? With this modest move White blunts the scope of the 'Scandinavian bishop', while the d4-square is left free for piece play. A timely ♘d4, further pestering the bishop, is certainly an option. Lines containing this idea are discussed in Chapter 4.

On g4 the bishop pins the knight on f3 to the white queen. Invariably White puts the question to the bishop with a swift h2-h3, when Black has to decide between ...♗xf3 and ...♗h5. Capturing the knight is only rarely in Black's plans, as one can easily drift into a passive, prospectless position after such an exchange.

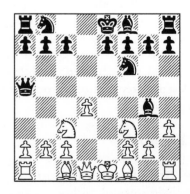

In this standard theoretical position Black players almost always play 6...♗h5, as after 6...♗xf3 7 ♕xf3 c6 8 ♗d2 e6 9 0-0-0, White has a free hand to attack with a kingside pawn launch with g2-g4-g5 and h2-h4, whereas Black, whilst giving the impression of having a solid position, has no visible signs of counterplay. These types of position are ideal for White and should normally be avoided by Black.

Going back to 6 h3 ♗h5, White often continues in an aggressive manner with 7 g4 ♗g6. Now the 'Scandinavian bishop' has returned to its favourite diagonal, but not before inducing h2-h3 and g2-g4. These pawn moves can sometimes prove to be weakening, but more often they help White to inaugurate a speedy assault on the kingside and in the centre. In particular, White's light-squared bishop finds an effective home at g2. These complex positions are the subject of Chapter 3.

Tactical Breaks

Since Black loses some time with the queen in the 2...♕xd5 variation, one has to be particularly careful in the opening moves. There are some nasty traps awaiting the unsuspecting player. One example occurs after the following plausible moves.

1 e4 d5 2 exd5 ♕xd5 3 ♘c3 ♕a5 4 d4 ♘f6 5 ♘f3 ♗f5 6 ♗d2 c6 7 ♗c4 ♘bd7 8 ♕e2

see following diagram

Black already faces some difficulties. It should first be pointed out that 8...♗xc2? is punished severely by 9

♘b5 ♕b6 10 ♘d6+ ♔d8 11 ♘xf7+. But what's wrong with 8...e6 here? Well, it looks solid enough, but White has the powerful breakthrough 9 d5! After 9...cxd5 10 ♘xd5 ♕d8 11 ♘xf6+ ♕xf6 12 0-0-0 White's lead in development has become much more significant due to the open nature of the position.

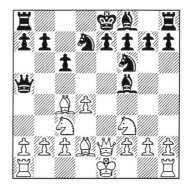

The following example is less complex, but still important.

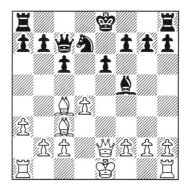

White has the bishop pair, which will thrive in an open position. 1 0-0 0-0 allows Black a abundantly comfortable game, as we shall see in Chapter 1. More testing is 1 d5! cxd5 2 ♗xd5 0-0 3 ♗f3, when the bishops have greatly increased their scope.

The Importance of ...♝b4

As early as Chapter 1 we shall learn the significance of an early ...♝b4.

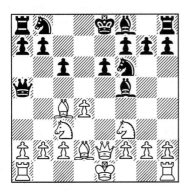

From the diagrammed position it has now been established that Black's best plan starts with 1...♝b4. Generally the bishop will trade itself for the knight on c3, leaving White with the bishop pair, but in return Black obtains more control over the light squares.

Domination of the Light Squares

One of Black's principal ideas in the Scandinavian Defence, particularly in the 2...♛d5 lines, is to take command of the light squares, using the queen, light-squared bishop, knights and also the pawns, which are predominately fixed on light squares.

---

see following diagram

In this position Danish Grandmaster Curt Hansen played the enlightening 1...♞b6 2 ♝b3 ♝xc3! 3 ♝xc3 ♛b5! 4 ♛xb5 cxb5 and Black soon obtained a fearsome bind on the light squares Notice the important squares e4, d5 and c4 are all under Black's control. See Game 2 for the rest of this instructive encounter.

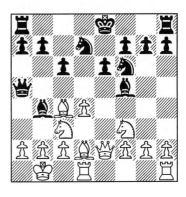

An Early b2-b4

The move b2-b4 is a typical attacking option for White, particularly when the black queen resides on a5 and the light-squared bishop has already moved.

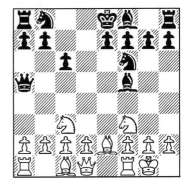

After 1 b4!? Black can either capture the pawn or retreat. In this position 1...♛xb4 2 ♖b1! turns out very well for White. The b7-pawn drops, after which White has simply managed to activate his queen's rook for no charge. If instead of snatching the pawn, the black queen retreats, say 1...♛c7, White can continue the offensive with 2 b5!

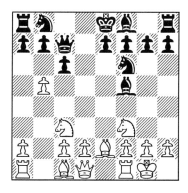

There are two ideas here. First, White is aiming to open up lines for his pieces, always a useful policy when slightly ahead in development. Second, there are some structural considerations. If Black captures on b5, or allows White to capture on c6 and then recaptures with a piece, then one of Black central prongs (i.e. the c6-pawn) disappears, and Black's control over the central squares decreases. If Black recaptures on c6 with the b-pawn, then this pawn itself will be isolated and may become weak, although Black can hope to liquidate this weakness with a timely ...c6-c5.

Sometimes b2-b4 can even be offered as a pawn sacrifice.

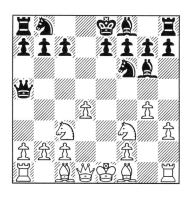

After 1 b4 ♕xb4 2 ♗d2 ♕d6 3 ♖b1 b6 4 ♗g2 c6 5 ♘e5 White's dynamic pieces offer him fantastic compensation for the pawn. Even here declining the pawn with 1...♕b6 is Black's most prudent option.

Castling
The 2...♕xd5 Scandinavian, more than most other openings, hands both players the chance to sharpen (or indeed pacify) the position with the choice of castling kingside or queenside. Take the following example.

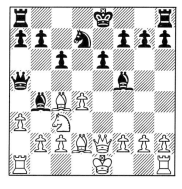

It is Black to move. The bishop on b4 is attacked, but there is no real threat at the moment due to the pin on a1-rook. Black can simply castle kingside or queenside, both options being perfectly acceptable. In return, after 1...0-0-0 or 1...0-0, White can reply 2 0-0 or 2 0-0-0(!). So in just one move all four castling configurations are possible.

b) 2...♘f6

Gambit Ideas
As I pointed out earlier, 2...♘f6 can entail more risk than 2...♕xd5, as

White does have ways of clasping hold of the pawn on d5, either for short-term nuisance value or with the plan of actually keeping the extra material for good. Because of this, Black players must sometimes be prepared to abandon attempts to reclaim material in favour of searching for active play as compensation. However, they can take heart in the fact there are many effective gambit ideas, which have the extra benefit of being good fun to play.

After 1 e4 d5 2 exd5 ♞f6 White's most obvious attempt to hang on to the material is with 3 c4. A fundamental gambit idea for Black is to play 3...c6!

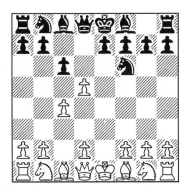

After 4 dxc6 ♞xc6 5 ♞f3 e5 Black's easy development and White's structural weakness more than compensate for the gambit pawn. As a result the large majority of White players refuse to touch this line and instead play 4 d4 cxd5 5 ♞c3, which transposes to the Caro-Kann, Panov-Botvinnik Attack (see Chapter 10).

More adventurous Black players may be attracted to the speculative Icelandic Gambit which arises after 1 e4 d5 2 exd5 ♞f6 3 c4 e6.

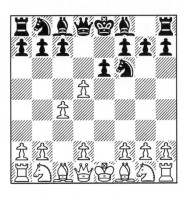

After 4 dxe6 ♝xe6 we have a gambit in the truest form: Black has some compensation for the pawn, but a lot of water has to pass under the bridge before we can safely come to an assessment (see Chapter 11).

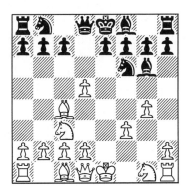

This position can arise from the 3 ♝b5+ variation. Black could try 1...♞bd7 in order to retrieve the pawn with ...♞bd7-b6-d5, but the most dynamic idea is 1...c6!? 2 dxc6 ♞xc6, when once again Black has visible compensation for the pawn.

Light Square Control
As with 2...♛xd5, Black can often hope to gain control of the light

squares, especially on the queenside. It sounds like a sweeping statement, but if Black is able to create some sort of light-squared bind, then he can often look forward to a comfortable game.

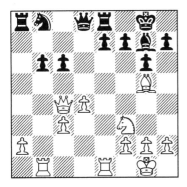

In this position 2...♘f6 expert Sergei Smagin played 16...b5! 17 ♕b3 ♖a4 18 ♘e5 ♗xe5!? 19 dxe5 ♘a6, and he was well on the way to mastering the light squares. After 20 ♖bd1 ♕c8 21 e6 f6! 22 ♗e3 ♘c7 23 ♖d7 ♖c4! it was clear that Black's bold strategy had paid dividends (see Game 41).

The d4/c4 Pawn Front

After the moves 1 e4 d5 2 exd5 ♘f6 3 d4 ♘xd5 4 c4 ♘b6 we reach a key position for the 2...♘f6 variation.

White's d4/c4 pawn front stands proudly in the centre, granting White a comfortable space edge. Sometimes one or both of the pawns may advance, possibly gaining time by attacking black pieces along the way. Of course White has to be careful in the handling of these assets. Negligence may well lead to them becoming a liability as opposed to a strength. In return Black has to play actively, or else risk being squashed in the centre. Black has at his disposal a few ways of combating White's centre:

a) ...g7-g6, ...♗g7, and ...0-0, followed by pressurising the d4-pawn with ...♘c6 and/or ...♗g4. Usually White is forced to advance one of the pawns, and Black hopes that the vacuum created in the centre can be occupied by his pieces.

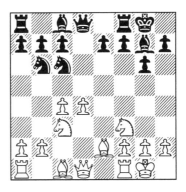

This is a typical theoretical position from Chapter 6. On 9 ♗e3 Black would step up the pressure on White's central pawns with 9...♗g4, while after 9 d5 ♘e5 10 ♘xe5 ♗xe5 White keeps the pawn centre, but the scope of Black's dark-squared bishop has been increased. Later on Black can nibble at White's centre with ...c7-c6 and ...e7-e6.

b) The same development idea as above, but aided with a pawn break in the centre, specifically ...e7-e5 or ...c7-c5. This idea is generally more effective when White has spent time on prophylactic moves such as h2-h3.

Here Black can strike with 9...e5! After 10 d5 ♘e7 Black has a strong foothold in the centre and the black pawn umbrella may open further with a timely ...f7-f5.

c) ...♗g4, followed by ...e7-e6, ...♗e7, ...0-0, and then a choice between ...♘c6 or ...c7-c5 and the more restrained ...c7-c6 and ...♘bd7. This is the least ambitious of Black's various set-ups.

The d4 Pawn Centre

Naturally White may also opt to exclude c2-c4 ideas in favour of keeping just one pawn in the central squares. One of the advantages of this restrained set-up is that the d4-pawn may be reinforced by c2-c3. This also gives more scope to White's pieces. For example the light-squared bishop has the option of the more active c4-square. Once again Black should be equipped to arrange an early strike at the centre. Pawn breaks are particularly important in these lines.

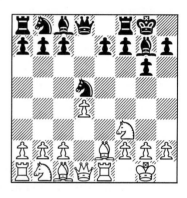

Here is another typical position from the 2...♘f6 variation. Here Black has the choice between 7...c6, followed by ...♘bd7, ...♕c7 and ...c7-c5 or ...e7-e5, and the more ambitious immediate 7...c5. After 8 dxc5 ♘a6 White can attempt to hold onto the extra pawn with 9 ♗xa6 bxa6, but we shall see in Chapter 7 that the open lines and the bishop pair grant Black some compensation.

CHAPTER ONE

2...♛xd5: The Main Line

---

1 e4 d5 2 exd5 ♛xd5 3 ♘c3 ♛a5 4 d4 ♘f6 5 ♘f3 ♗f5 6 ♗d2 c6 7 ♗c4 e6 8 ♛e2

The position after 1 e4 d5 2 exd5 ♛xd5 3 ♘c3 ♛a5 4 d4 ♘f6 5 ♘f3 ♗f5 6 ♗d2 c6 7 ♗c4 e6 8 ♛e2 is one of the most common in the 2...♛xd5 Scandinavian, and can be considered to be the main line. Considered simply as 'good for White' by the heavyweight opening bible *ECO*, Black players shied away from this variation for many years. The last decade, however, has seen an outbreak of new ideas and games. During that time Black's theoretical standing and practical results have improved significantly. Indeed, many White players have started searching for fresh ideas in other variations (see Chapters 2-4) and it is even conceivable that this variation will lose its 'main line' tag in the future.

After the almost universally played 8...♗b4, White generally chooses between 9 0-0-0 (Games 1-3) and 9 ♘e5 (Games 4-7). Both continuations may lead to both sharp and positional battles, although 9 0-0-0 is considered to be the more dynamic try.

From the Black point of view, it is

a particularly good idea to study the games of Danish Grandmaster Curt Hansen from this chapter. Hansen, more than anyone, has promoted Black's counter-chances in this variation, and has shown that it is possible to win with Black in both a tactical and positional manner.

> *Game 1*
> **Nijboer-Hodgson**
> *Dutch Team Championship 1995*

1 e4 d5 2 exd5 ♛xd5 3 ♘c3 ♛a5 4 d4 c6 5 ♘f3 ♘f6 6 ♗c4 ♗f5 7 ♛e2 e6 8 ♗d2 ♗b4

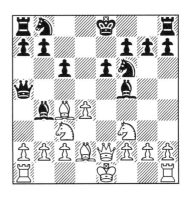

A fundamental idea in the main line, cutting out any of White's basic tricks involving d4-d5 or ♘d5. The

---

risky 8...♘bd7 9 d5! is considered (by transposition) in Game 8.

9 0-0-0

Castling on the queen's wing is White's most energetic continuation. For 9 ♘e5 see Games 4-8.

9...♘bd7

The slightly risky 9...♘d5 is dealt with in Game 3.

10 a3

White's alternatives here are considered in the next game.

10...♗xc3

It is important to note that Black must usually be prepared to exchange on c3 with this bishop. In this position sacrifices don't work. After 10...♗xa3? 11 ♘a2! (a customary refutation of ...♗xa3 ideas) 11...♗xb2+ 12 ♔xb2 ♕b6+ 13 ♔c1 White's king is a little draughty, but it is well defended by pieces and Black does not have sufficient firepower to mount a serious attack.

11 ♗xc3 ♕c7 12 ♘e5 ♘xe5

12...♘d5 did not work out well in Sveshnikov-Lastin, Elista 1995. That game continued 13 ♗d2 b5 14 ♗b3 ♘xe5 15 dxe5 0-0-0 16 g4 ♗g6 17 f4 h5 18 h3 a6 19 ♕f3!, and the dangerous threat of f5 forced Black to play 19...f5 himself, although after 20 exf6 gxf6 21 ♖he1 hxg4 22 hxg4 e5 23 f5 ♗f7 24 ♖h1 ♖he8 25 ♕e4! ♖d7 26 g5 the position had opened up favourably for White's two bishops.

12...b5, although slightly weakening, does have the merit of securing the outpost on d5 for the f6-knight. There are then two ways for White to proceed:

a) 13 ♗d3 0-0! (13...♗xd3?! only al-

lows White to swing the rook across the third rank with 14 ♖xd3 0-0 15 ♖g3!) 14 ♗xf5 exf5 15 ♕f3! ♘d5! 16 ♕xf5 ♘xc3 17 ♘xd7 (or 17 bxc3 ♘b6 18 ♖d3 ♕e7 19 ♔b2 ♖ac8 and White's airy king balances out the extra pawn) 17...♘xd1 18 ♘xf8 ♖xf8 19 ♖xd1 (19 ♔xd1 ♖d8 20 ♕e4 c5 is level) 19...♕xh2, and in this equal position the players agreed a draw in Almasi-Dautov, Altensteig 1994.

b) 13 ♗b3 ♗e4 14 ♖he1 and now best for Black is 14...♘d5, as the tempting 15 ♘xf7? fails to 15...♔xf7 16 ♗xd5 exd5 17 ♕e7+ ♔g6 18 ♖d3 ♖he8 19 ♖g3+ ♕xg3!, when Black wins.

13 dxe5 ♘d5 14 ♗d2 0-0-0 15 g4 ♗g6 16 f4

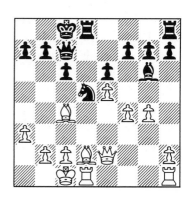

A typical plan. White's objective is to achieve f4-f5, crowding out the black bishop. Black needs to respond actively.

16...h5 17 h3 ♕b6!? 18 ♖hf1 hxg4 19 hxg4 ♖h3!?

In the stem game Psakhis-Wahls, Baden Baden 1992, the German Grandmaster tried 19...♕c5 20 ♗b3 (20 f5? is premature: 20...exf5 21 gxf5 ♗h5!) 20...♖h3 21 ♖f3 ♖dh8 22 ♖df1

♖h2 23 ♕e1! ♕d4 (but not 23...♖g2? 24 f5 exf5 25 gxf5 ♖hh2 26 fxg6 ♖xd2 27 ♕xd2! ♖xd2 28 gxf7 and White wins) 24 f5 exf5 25 gxf5 ♗h5 26 ♖d3 ♕g4. Now instead of 27 ♗xd5 Psakhis recommends 27 c4 as giving a small edge for White.

20 ♖de1?!

I prefer the direct 20 f5! exf5 (20...♗h7 21 ♕g2 is better for White) 21 gxf5 (21 e6 also looks interesting) 21...♗h5 22 ♕g2 ♖h4 23 ♗xd5 ♖xd5 24 ♖de1, when White's centralised pieces offer a modest advantage.

20...♕d4 21 ♗a2?

21 ♗b3 had to be played, but Nijboer had missed Hodgson's dazzling reply.

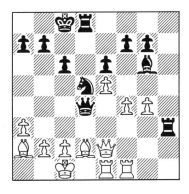

21...♖xa3!!

A bolt from the blue, which completely ruins White's position.

22 ♗b1

22 bxa3 ♕a1+ 23 ♗b1 ♕xa3+ 24 ♔d1 ♘c3 is a very pleasing mate.

22...♕a4 23 f5 ♖a1 24 c3

Or 24 c4 exf5 25 gxf5 ♗h5 26 ♕xh5 ♕xc4+ 27 ♗c3 ♕d3 and White cannot prevent checkmate.

24...exf5 25 gxf5 ♗h5 26 ♕xh5 ♕a2 27 ♔c2 ♕c4!

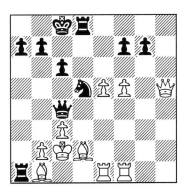

After this 'quiet move' there is absolutely no way out of the net.

28 b3

Or 28 ♕xf7 ♘b4+ 29 ♔c1 ♕d3.

28...♘b4+ 29 ♔c1 ♖xb1+ 0-1

Since 29...♖xb1+ 30 ♔xb1 ♕xb3+ 31 ♔a1 ♘c2 is mate. A sparkling attack by Hodgson and a good illustration of Black's counter-chances in this line.

> *Game 2*
> **Hjartarson-C.Hansen**
> *Reykjavik 1995*

1 e4 d5 2 exd5 ♕xd5 3 ♘c3 ♕a5 4 d4 ♘f6 5 ♘f3 ♗f5 6 ♗c4 e6 7 ♗d2 c6 8 ♕e2 ♗b4 9 0-0-0 ♘bd7 10 ♔b1

One must also consider the direct 10 ♘h4, in order to exchange the 'Scandinavian bishop'. White must pay a price for this trade, as following 10...♗g4 11 f3 ♗xc3! he is forced to capture with the b-pawn (12 ♗xc3 allows 12...♕g5+). After 12 bxc3 ♗h5 we have two examples:

a) 13 g4 ♗g6 14 ♗b3 ♕a3+ 15 ♔b1 a5! 16 ♘f5 a4 17 ♘xg7+ ♔d8 18 ♗c1 ♕f8 19 ♗h6 axb3! 20 ♘xe6+ fxe6 21

♗xf8 bxc2+ 22 ♔a1 cxd1♕+ 23 ♖xd1 ♖xf8, as in Rytshagov-Westerinen, Parnu 1996. Black's material advantage should be decisive, although the game was finally drawn.

b) 13 ♗b3 0-0-0 14 ♔b2 ♕c7 15 g4 ♗g6 16 ♘g2 h5?! (16...h6! is stronger, as after 16...h5 Black is rather tied up) 17 g5 ♘g8 18 ♗f4 ♕a5 19 ♘e3 ♘b6 20 ♗e5! ♖h7 21 ♘c4 ♘xc4+ 22 ♕xc4 ♘e7 23 ♕e2 ♘d5 24 ♕e1 ♘b6?! (24...h4!) 25 c4 ♕xe1 26 ♖hxe1 and White had a significant advantage in Smagin-Levin, Novgorod 1995.

10...♘b6 11 ♗b3

11...♗xc3!? 12 ♗xc3 ♕b5

A rather surprising concept. Black offers the exchange of queens, accepting a pair of doubled pawns into the bargain. But far from being weak, this structure actually helps Black to clamp down on the queenside in the resulting endgame.

13 ♕xb5 cxb5 14 ♘e5 a5 15 a3 ♗e4 16 ♖he1 0-0 17 f3 ♗d5 18 ♗xd5 ♘fxd5 19 ♗d2 ♘c4 20 ♗c1 ♖fc8

Black has achieved complete domination over the light squares on the queenside. The knight on d5 cannot

be displaced and White's bishop remains a spectator. All in all, the opening has been a complete success for Black.

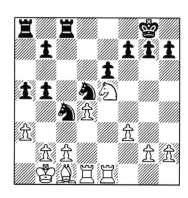

21 f4 b4 22 ♘xc4 ♖xc4 23 ♖d3 bxa3 24 ♖xa3 b5 25 f5 b4 26 ♖d3 exf5 27 ♖e5 ♖d8 28 ♖xf5 a4 29 ♗d2 f6 30 h3 ♔f7 31 g4 g6 32 ♖ff3 ♖e8 33 c3 ♖e2 34 cxb4 ♘xb4 35 ♖c3 ♖xd4 36 ♖c7+ ♔e6 37 ♗c1 ♖d1 38 ♖cc3 ♖ed2 39 ♖f4 ♘d3 40 ♖c6+ ♔d5 41 ♖fxf6 ♖xb2+ 42 ♔a1 ♖b5 43 ♖fd6+ ♔e5 0-1

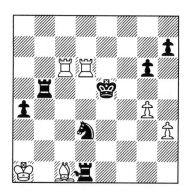

After 44 ♖e6+ ♔d4 45 ♖ed6+ ♖d5 Black wins a piece. A very instructive game from Curt Hansen, who is a real champion of Black's prospects in this variation.

1 e4 d5 2 exd5 ♕xd5 3 ♘c3 ♕a5 4 ♘f3 ♘f6 5 d4 ♗f5 6 ♗d2 c6 7 ♗c4 e6 8 ♕e2 ♗b4 9 0-0-0 ♘d5!?

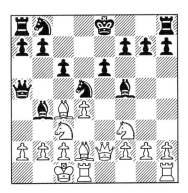

9...♘d5 earned a dubious reputation following this game and it is hardly ever played nowadays. However, things may not be as clear cut as was first thought.

10 ♘xd5 ♗xd2+ 11 ♘xd2 cxd5 12 ♘b3 ♕xa2

12...♕d8 is an important alternative. After 13 ♗b5+ Black has a choice:

a) 13...♔e7 looks unappetising. Following 14 g4 ♗g6 15 f4 a6 16 ♗d3 ♗xd3 17 ♖xd3 ♖e8 18 ♖h3 h6 19 ♖f1 ♔f8 20 g5 hxg5 21 ♖h8+ ♔e7 22 ♖h7 ♘d7 23 fxg5 ♖g8 24 ♕f2 White was clearly better in Morawietz-Wacker, Germany 1995.

b) I can't find too much wrong with the sensible 13...♘c6. White can try 14 ♘c5 but after 14...♕g5+! 15 ♕d2 (15 ♔b1 0-0 16 ♘xb7 ♘b4 17 ♗a4 ♕xg2 looks okay for Black)

15...♕xd2+ 16 ♖xd2 0-0-0 Black's position is perfectly acceptable.

13 ♗xd5 ♘c6 14 g4 ♗g6 15 ♗xc6+ bxc6 16 f4 0-0 17 h4 h6 18 h5 ♗h7 19 g5 ♗f5 20 gxh6 gxh6 21 ♖hg1+ ♔h7 22 ♖g3 ♖g8 23 ♖dg1 ♖xg3 24 ♖xg3

24...a5?

This just loses a pawn. The superior 24...♕a4! was played in the correspondence game Grabowicz-Dziel. After 25 ♕e5 ♖g8 26 ♖xg8 ♔xg8 White decided that there was nothing better than 27 ♕b8+ ♔g7 28 ♕e5+ ♔g8 29 ♕b8+ ♔g7 with a draw by perpetual check.

25 ♕e5 ♖g8 26 ♖xg8 ♔xg8 27 ♕xa5 ♕xa5 28 ♘xa5 ♗e4 29 ♔d2 ♔g7 30 c4 ♔f6 31 ♔e3 ♗h1 32 b4 ♔f5 33 b5 cxb5 34 cxb5 f6 35 ♘c4 ♔g4 36 ♘d6 ♗a8 37 b6 ♔xh5 38 f5 e5 39 dxe5 fxe5 40 b7 ♗xb7 41 ♘xb7 1-0

1 e4 d5 2 exd5 ♕xd5 3 ♘c3 ♕a5 4 d4 ♘f6 5 ♘f3 ♗f5 6 ♗c4 c6 7 ♗d2

e6 8 ♕e2 ♝b4 9 ♘e5 ♘bd7

As one might expect, 9...♝xc2? would be punished swiftly with 10 ♘xf7! ♚xf7 11 ♕xe6+ ♚g6 12 ♕f7+ ♚f5 13 ♝e6 mate.

10 0-0-0!?

The usual move is 10 ♘xd7 (see Games 5-7).

10...♘xe5 11 dxe5 ♘d5!

After 11...♘d7 12 a3! Black has a choice of two evils:

a) 12...♝xc3 13 ♝xc3 ♕c7 14 ♖d6 and Black is extremely confined.

b) 12...b5 13 ♝a2 ♝xa3 14 bxa3 ♕xa3+ 15 ♚b1 0-0 16 ♝c1 ♕b4+ 17 ♝b2 and Black did not really have enough play for the piece in Jansa-Taulbut Copenhagen 1981, although the English IM did go on to win.

12 ♝xd5 exd5 13 g4

13 a3 runs straight into 13...♝xa3!, as Judit Polgar found out when she tested it against the Scandinavian authority Curt Hansen in Groningen 1993. After 14 ♕f3 ♝e6 15 ♘a2 ♝b4! 16 ♝xb4 ♕xa2 17 ♕e3 0-0-0 Hansen was clearly on top, although Polgar did manage to scrape a draw in the end.

13...d4!

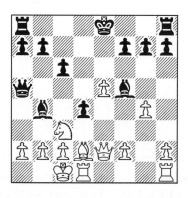

Introduced by Taylor as an improvement over 13...♝e6 and 13...♝d7, 13...d4 seems to give Black at least equality.

14 ♘b1 ♝e6 15 a3 ♝xd2+ 16 ♖xd2

16 ♘xd2 also promises little. After 16...0-0 Taylor has had a couple of encounters:

a) 17 f4 b5 18 f5 ♝d5 19 ♖he1 b4 20 ♘b1 c5 21 f6 bxa3 22 ♘xa3 ♖ab8 23 fxg7 ♖fe8 24 ♖d3 c4 25 ♖xd4 ♖xb2! 26 ♘xc4 (26 ♚xb2 c3+) 26...♝xc4 27 ♖xc4 ♖a2 and White had to resign in Shannon-Taylor, 1988.

b) 17 ♖hg1 d3! (watch out for this theme) 18 ♕xd3 ♕xe5 19 ♖de1 ♕a5 20 ♘b3 ♕b6 21 ♖e3 ♖ad8 22 ♕e2 c5 and the bishop versus knight on an open board ensures a slight pull for Black, Pedersen-Taylor, USA 1990.

16...0-0-0 17 f4 c5 18 ♖dd1 ♕a4 19 ♘d2?

Missing Black's next move. White should have played the direct 19 f5! ♝c4 20 ♕f2 ♝d5 21 ♖he1, with chances for both sides.

19...d3!

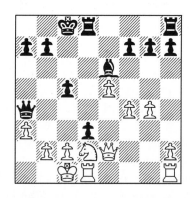

A second important move by this pawn gives Black a won position, as White is saddled with weak pawns on d3 and e5.

20 cxd3 ♕xf4 21 h3 ♖d5 22 ♖de1 ♖hd8 23 ♖hf1 ♕h6 24 ♖f3 c4! 25 ♔b1 cxd3 26 ♕f2 ♔b8 27 ♖fe3 ♕g5 28 ♕g3 ♕g6 29 h4 ♖d4 30 g5 ♕h5 0-1

I suppose that White could have struggled on for a while longer, but in correspondence chess this would have been a depressing and ultimately fruitless course of action.

Game 5
Van der Wiel-C.Hansen
Wijk aan Zee 1993

---

1 e4 d5 2 exd5 ♕xd5 3 ♘c3 ♕a5 4 d4 ♘f6 5 ♘f3 ♗f5 6 ♗c4 e6 7 ♗d2 c6 8 ♕e2 ♗b4 9 ♘e5 ♘bd7 10 ♘xd7 ♘xd7

The alternative recapture, 10...♔xd7, is considered in Game 7.

11 a3

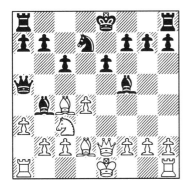

11...0-0

The solid choice. For the more adventurous 11...0-0-0 see Game 6. In any case it is useful for Black to delay ...♗xc3 for one move. The immediate 11...♗xc3 is less accurate as after 12 ♗xc3 ♕c7 White has the extra possibility of 13 d5!?, opening the game up for the bishop pair. Following 13...cxd5 14 ♗xd5 0-0 15 ♗f3 we have two branches:

a) 15...♖ac8 16 0-0 ♘b6 17 ♖ac1 ♖fd8 18 ♖fd1 ♖xd1+ 19 ♖xd1 h6 (19...♘a4 20 ♗e5 ♕xc2 21 ♕xc2 ♗xc2 22 ♖c1 ♖c5 23 ♗d6 ♖c4 24 ♗d1 wins for White) and now instead of 20 ♖c1 ♘c4! with equal chances (Vogt-Dautov, Altensteig 1994), Dautov recommends 20 h4! ♘a4 21 ♗e5 ♕b6 22 ♗d4 ♕c7 23 c4! with a plus for White, as 23...♕xc4 fails to 24 ♕xc4 ♖xc4 25 b3, winning a piece.

b) 15...♘f6 16 ♗e5! ♕xc2 17 ♕xc2 ♗xc2 18 ♗xb7 ♖ad8 19 0-0 ♗b3 20 ♖ac1 and the two bishops ensured a pleasant endgame for White in Tischbierek-Doncevic, Germany 1991.

It is interesting to note that both *ECO* and *BCO* give this whole variation a very bad press, as far as Black is concerned. Both sources quote only the unnecessary 11...♘b6?! here, which was played in the game Chandler-Rogers, Bath 1983. After 12 0-0 ♘xc4 13 axb4 ♕xb4 14 ♖a4!, White won a piece. But what about simple moves such as 11...0-0 and 11...0-0-0?

12 0-0-0 ♗xc3 13 ♗xc3 ♕c7 14 ♗d3 ♘f6!

see following diagram

Compare Hansen's strategy here to his encounter with Hjartarson (Game 2). The Danish GM once again freely accepts doubled pawns in return for some light-square control.

15 ♗xf5 ♕f4+ 16 ♔b1 exf5 17 ♗d2 ♕e4 18 ♕xe4 fxe4 19 ♖he1 ♖fe8 20 ♖e2 b5 21 ♖de1 ♖ad8 22 c3

♖e6 23 ♗g5!

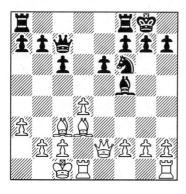

Not allowing Black to consolidate with ...♖de8 and ...♘d5.

23...h6 24 ♗xf6 ♖xf6 25 ♖xe4 ♖xf2 26 ♖1e2 ½-½

Game 6
Vogt-Wahls
Swiss Open Championship 1994

---

1 e4 d5 2 exd5 ♕xd5 3 ♘c3 ♕a5 4 d4 c6 5 ♘f3 ♘f6 6 ♗d2 ♗f5 7 ♗c4 e6 8 ♕e2 ♗b4 9 ♘e5 ♘bd7 10 ♘xd7 ♘xd7 11 a3 0-0-0

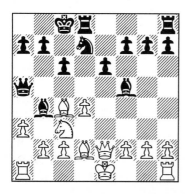

More daring than 11...0-0, but at the same time more hazardous, as White may be able to launch an attack with the queenside pawns.

12 0-0

After 12 0-0-0 Black can opt for the safe 12...♗xc3 13 ♗xc3 ♕c7 or try the complex 12...♗xa3!? The game Britton-Prie, London-Paris 1994, continued 13 bxa3 (after 13 ♘a2 ♕a4 14 ♗b3 ♕xd4! 15 ♗c3 ♕f4+ 16 ♗d2 Black can either take a draw with 16...♕d4 or enter an unclear endgame with 16...♕e4 17 ♕xe4 ♗xb2+ 18 ♔xb2 ♗xe4, the three pawns balancing White's extra piece) 13...♕xa3+ 14 ♔b1 ♘b6 (14...♕b4+!?) 15 ♘a2 ♕a4 16 ♗d3 ♗xd3 17 ♕xd3 ♖xd4 18 ♕b3 ♖hd8

19 ♕xa4 ♘xa4 20 ♔c1 c5 21 ♗e3 ♖xd1+ 22 ♖xd1 ♖d5 23 ♖d3 ♖xd3 24 cxd3 ♔d7 and the French GM went on to win, although at this stage the ending is still very complicated.

12...♗xc3 13 ♗xc3 ♕c7 14 b4

As this lunge does not have the desired effect, perhaps White should consider the quieter 14 ♖fd1, preparing to meet 14...♘b6 15 ♗b3 ♘d5 with 16 ♗d2.

14...♘f6

This position is really quite deceptive. At first sight it appears as if White may be able to drum up a quick offensive on the queenside. Closer inspection, however, reveals that the white bishops have little scope and their presence actually impedes the attack. Furthermore, there is still that nagging pressure on the c2-pawn, while the 'Scandinavian bishop' and knight are functioning well together. I would not go as far as to say that Black is better, but it is certainly a very comfortable position for him to play.

15 f3 ♘d5 16 ♗b2 ♘f4 17 ♕e3?

White goes 'all in' by off-loading his Achilles' heel. It soon becomes apparent, however, that Black's position is extremely resolute. After the more sober 17 ♕d2 Black can ensure counterplay with 17...♖hg8, preparing ...g7-g5.

17...♗xc2 18 ♖fc1 ♗f5 19 b5 ♘d5 20 ♗xd5 ♖xd5 21 bxc6 bxc6 22 ♖c4 ♔d7!

The monarch is very well protected here and Black's bishop on f5 ensures that White cannot dominate the b-file.

23 ♗c3 ♖b8 24 ♗e1 ♖b1 25 ♖xb1 ♗xb1 26 ♗g3 ♕b6 27 h3 ♗a2 28 ♖c2 ♕b1+ 29 ♖c1 ♕b6 30 ♖d1 c5! 31 ♕f4 ♔e8 32 ♖c1 c4!

Black has consolidated completely and this passed pawn will be a constant thorn in White's flesh.

33 ♔h2 h6 34 ♕d2 ♗b3 35 ♗f2 ♕d6+ 36 ♗g3 ♕xa3 37 ♕f4 ♕a5 38 ♕b8+ ♖d8 39 ♕f4 ♔f8 40 ♖b1 ♔g8

Who would have guessed that Black castled queenside earlier on?

41 ♕e3 ♕d5 42 ♗f2 a5 43 ♔g1 a4 44 ♖a1 ♕d6 45 ♕c1 ♖a8 46 ♕e3 ♖d8 47 ♕c1 ♕b4 48 ♗e1 ♕b6 49 ♗f2 ♖d5 50 f4 ♕c7 0-1

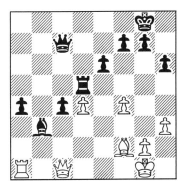

White can only prevent ...c4-c3 by dropping another pawn. An efficient display by Wahls and an excellent example of the resilience in Black's position.

> *Game 7*
> **Emms-Ryan**
> *British Championship 1992*

1 e4 d5 2 exd5 ♕xd5 3 ♘c3 ♕a5 4 d4 ♘f6 5 ♘f3 ♗f5 6 ♗c4 e6 7 ♗d2 c6 8 ♕e2 ♗b4 9 ♘e5 ♘bd7 10 ♘xd7 ♔xd7!?

Another idea of Taylor's. The f6-knight has not been displaced and Black intends ...♖ad8 and ...♔c8 to 'castle queenside by hand'. However, it transpires that 10...♞xd7 and 10...♚xd7 are in fact very closely linked (see the note to Black's 14th).

11 0-0-0 ♖ad8 12 a3 ♝xc3 13 ♝xc3 ♛c7 14 f3 ♚c8

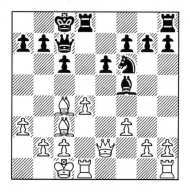

Counting up the tempi, we discover that this position could have also arisen via the move-order 10...♞xd7 11 a3 0-0-0 12 0-0-0 ♝xc3 13 ♝xc3 ♛c7 14 f3 ♞f6.

15 g4 ♝g6 16 ♝e1!

A powerful manoeuvre. The bishop will be very well placed on g3.

16...♞d5?!

After the game we both decided that 16...b5, securing the d5-outpost for the knight, is a better alternative here. After 17 ♝b3 ♖d7 18 ♝g3 ♛b6 the position is roughly level. White may have the token advantage of the two bishops, but Black's minor pieces are also well placed and his position is extremely difficult to breach.

17 ♝g3 ♛b6 18 ♖he1 ♖he8 19 h4 h5 20 ♝d3! hxg4 21 ♝xg6 gxf3 22 ♛xf3 fxg6 23 ♛g4 ♞f6 24 ♛xg6

At this stage I was extremely content with my position. The bishop on g3 dominates the knight and Black's e6- and g7-pawns are very fragile.

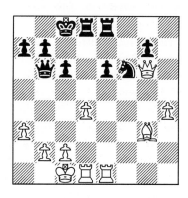

24...♖xd4 25 ♛xg7 ♖g4?

25...♖xd1+ 26 ♖xd1 e5, planning to meet 27 ♛xf6 with 27...♛e3+ and 28...♛xg3, would have been more stubborn. However, White still maintains a substantial advantage with the simple 27 ♖e1, as the passed h-pawn will obviously become an important player.

26 ♛xf6 ♖xg3 27 ♖xe6 ♖e3 28 ♖xe8+ ♖xe8 29 h5

This mighty passed pawn decides.

29...♛e3+ 30 ♚b1 ♛e2 31 ♛f5+ ♚b8 32 ♖h1 ♛g2 33 ♖h3 ♖e1+ 34 ♚a2 ♛g1 35 ♛f4+ ♚c8 36 h6 ♛g8+ 37 c4 ♛h7 38 ♛g4+ ♚d8 39 ♛d4+

In time-trouble I missed the simpler 39 ♛h4+ ♖e7 40 ♖e3. Fortunately I received a second chance three moves later.

39...♚c7 40 ♛f4+ ♚c8 41 ♛g4+ ♚d8 42 ♛h4+! ♖e7 43 ♖e3 1-0

> *Game 8*
> **Spassky-Larsen**
> *Montreal 1979*

1 e4 d5 2 exd5 ♛xd5 3 ♞c3 ♛a5 4 d4 ♞f6 5 ♞f3 ♝f5 6 ♝d2 ♞bd7 7 ♝c4 c6 8 ♛e2 e6

Not surprisingly 8...♗xc2 fails, to 9 ♘b5, followed by ♘d6+.

9 d5!

The insertion of ...♘bd7 at the expense of ...♗b4 has one important drawback, and this breakthrough is exactly it.

9...cxd5 10 ♘xd5 ♕c5

This move has been criticised, but in my opinion Black is struggling in any case. Some sources give 10...♕d8 as a major improvement. After 11 ♘xf6+ ♕xf6 (11...gxf6 may be a tougher defence, but of course White must still have a sizeable edge after 12 ♘d4) I offer the following lines:

a) 12 ♗c3 ♗b4!? 13 ♗xb4 ♕xb2 14 0-0 ♕xb4 15 ♗b5 0-0-0 16 ♖ab1 with a strong initiative for the pawn. For example, 16...♕e4 17 ♕d2 ♘c5 18 ♕a5! a6 19 ♖b4 ♕d5 20 ♖d4! or 16...♕a5 17 ♘d4 ♘b6 18 ♕e5! (threatening ♗d7+) 18...♕xa2 19 ♖b3 ♘d5 20 ♘xf5 exf5 21 ♗c4, both of which lead to winning positions for White.

b) 12 0-0-0! is even stronger, placing Black in deep trouble over the threats of ♗g5 and ♗b5. After 12...♗a3!? 13 c3 ♗e7 (13...♗c5 has been approved by a couple of sources, but it just loses to 14 ♗g5 ♕g6 15 ♖xd7!) 14 ♗b5 e5 15 ♗g5 ♕xg5+ 16 ♘xg5 ♗xg5+ 17 ♖d2 Black has no compensation for the material deficit.

11 b4 ♕c8 12 ♘xf6+ gxf6

Not a pleasant move to have to make, but 12...♘xf6 13 ♗b5+ ♔e7 (13...♘d7? 14 ♘e5) 14 ♘d4 ♗g6 15 0-0 presents White with the powerful plan of f2-f4-f5.

13 ♘d4 ♗g6 14 h4 h5 15 f4! ♗e7 16 ♖h3 ♕c7

White has a indisputable advantage owing to his lead in development, Black's shaky pawn structure and also Black's insecure king. Indeed, whichever way the black king journeys, he runs straight into trouble: 16...0-0 17 f5 exf5 18 ♖g3! ♔h7 19 ♘xf5 is murderous.

17 0-0-0 ♕b6 18 ♗e1 0-0-0 19 ♘b5!

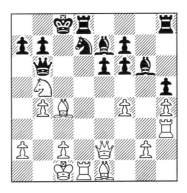

All of White's army, including the two rooks, have reached very active posts. Meanwhile the black king still looks unstable. The rest is carnage.

19...♘b8 20 ♖xd8+! ♔xd8

Or 20...♖xd8 21 ♗f2.

21 ♗f2 ♕c6 22 ♗xa7 ♘d7 23 a3 ♕e4 24 ♗e3 ♗f5 25 ♖g3 ♕c6 26 ♘d4 ♕a4 27 ♘xf5! ♕xa3+ 28 ♔d1 ♕a1+ 29 ♗c1 ♗xb4

29...exf5 runs into 30 ♖a3! ♕d4+ 31 ♖d3, when 31...♕xc4 allows 32 ♖xd7+ ♔xd7 33 ♕xc4.

30 ♗b5 ♘b6 31 ♕e4 ♕a5 32 ♕xb7 1-0

As 32...♕xb5 33 ♖d3+ ♔e8 34 ♕b8+ ♘c8 35 ♕xc8 is mate.

Summary

The onus is really on White to come up with something fresh and challenging in these main lines. Perhaps 9 0-0-0 ♘bd7 10 a3 and 10 ♘h4 are White's best tries for an edge, but this doesn't alter the fact that basically Black has a very sound position.

1 e4 d5 2 exd5 ♕xd5 3 ♘c3 ♕a5 4 d4 ♘f6 5 ♘f3 ♗f5 6 ♗d2 c6 7 ♗c4 e6 8 ♕e2

8...♗b4 *(D)*
      8...♘bd7 - *game 8*
9 0-0-0
      9 ♘e5 ♘bd7
            10 0-0-0 - *game 4*
            10 ♘xd7
                 10...♘xd7 11 a3 *(D)*
                       11...0-0 - *game 5*
                       11...0-0-0 - *game 6*
                 10...♚xd7 - *game 7*
9...♘bd7 *(D)*
      (9...♘d5 - *game 3*)
10 a3 - *game 1*
10 ♚b1 - *game 2*

    8...♗b4   *11 a3*   *9...♘bd7*

CHAPTER TWO

2...♛xd5: Main Line Alternatives

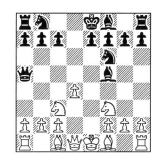

1 e4 d5 2 exd5 ♛xd5 3 ♘c3 ♛a5 4 d4 ♞f6 5 ♞f3 ♝f5

As I mentioned in Chapter 1, since Black's revival in the line 1 e4 d5 2 exd5 ♛xd5 3 ♘c3 ♛a5 4 d4 ♞f6 5 ♞f3 ♝f5 6 ♝d2 c6 7 ♝c4 e6 8 ♛e2 ♝b4!, White players have been forced to search for different ways and means to present Black with problems. In this section we shall examine White's main alternatives at moves six, seven and eight.

Games 9 and 10 see White resolving the early tension with 6 ♝d2 c6 7 ♝c4 e6 8 ♘d5. After the forced 8...♛d8 9 ♘xf6+ Black may recapture with g-pawn or queen. Capturing with the pawn gives a position reminiscent of a ...gxf6 Caro-Kann (1 e4 c6 2 d4 d5 3 ♘c3 dxe4 4 ♘xe4 ♞f6 5 ♘xf6+ gxf6). 9...♛xf6 is also perfectly playable, although in both lines there are a few pitfalls to beware of.

The most significant option is probably 6 ♘e5 (Games 11-13), giving White the chance of an early g2-g4. Black has to be particularly careful in this line, as White frequently obtains dangerous attacking chances on the kingside. Nevertheless, if Black is able to weather the early storm, his chances of success are good, as these pawn moves may leave White over-stretched.

Naturally White can also play in a restrained manner, castling kingside and sometimes reserving the option of ♘e5. We shall discuss these quiet ideas in Games 14-15.

Game 9
Emms-Conquest
Montecatini Terme 1996

---

1 e4 d5 2 exd5 ♛xd5 3 ♘c3 ♛a5 4 ♞f3 ♞f6 5 d4 ♝f5 6 ♝d2 c6 7 ♝c4 e6 8 ♘d5

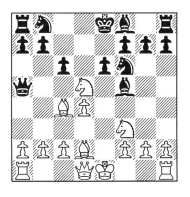

8...♛d8 9 ♘xf6+ ♛xf6
For 9...gxf6 see Game 10.
10 ♘e5

The only way to justify White's earlier play. After the pedestrian 10 0-0 ♘d7! Black has a very comfortable game.

10...♘d7!

An excellent move. Against the 10...♗d6 I had planned the straightforward 11 0-0!, when Black can grab a pawn but may suffer a great deal on the dark squares: 11...♗xe5 12 dxe5 ♕xe5 13 ♗c3 ♕c5 14 ♕e2 0-0 15 b4! ♕e7 16 ♖ad1 (or 16 ♕e5!?) is quite unpleasant for Black, as the natural 16...♘d7 runs into 17 ♖xd7! ♕xd7 18 ♕e5 f6 19 ♕xf5. Declining the offer with 10...♗d6 11 0-0 ♘bd7 allows White to prop up the knight with 12 f4.

11 ♘xd7 ♕xd4!?

This is not necessarily bad, but it is unnecessarily risky. The dependable alternative 11...♔xd7 12 c3 gives Black a perfectly playable position, despite the loss of the right to castle, e.g.

a) 12...♕g6 13 0-0 ♗e4 (13...♗d6 14 ♖e1 h5 15 ♗f1! h4 16 ♕f3 ♕f6?! 17 ♕e3 ♖ag8?! 18 c4! b6 19 a4 g5 20 a5 and White's attack was much quicker in Emms-Haveland, Gausdal [Troll Masters] 1996) 14 f3 ♗c2 15 ♕c1 ♗d6 and Black has no problems.

b) 12...♗d6 13 0-0 ♕h4! (forcing White to weaken his kingside) 14 g3 ♕h3 15 ♖e1 h5 16 ♗f1 ♕g4 17 ♕b3!? ♔c7 18 ♗e2 ♕g6 19 c4 h4 20 c5 ♗e7 21 ♗f4+ ♔c8 22 ♗f3 hxg3 23 hxg3 ♕h7 and Black is certainly no worse in the complications.

12 ♕e2!

This move was underestimated by my opponent. In fact, 12 ♕e2 is prac-tically forced as the alternative 12 ♘xf8 is actually better for Black after 12 ♘xf8 ♕xc4 13 ♘xe6 ♕xe6+ 14 ♗e3 ♕g6!

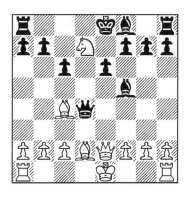

12...♕xd7 13 0-0-0 ♗e7?

Here Stuart decided to off-load his extra pawn in order to activate his remaining pieces. This was an under-standable reaction, but incorrect nev-ertheless. After the game we decided that Black has two more testing alter-natives.

a) 13...h5!? slows down White's kingside pawn storm, not fearing pos-sible discovered attacks on the black queen. White should probably con-tinue 14 ♗f4 ♕c8 15 f3 and play for g2-g4 in any case.

b) 13...♕c7 is the most natural move, removing the queen from the d-file. Against this I had planned 14 g4 ♗g6 15 h4 h5 16 ♗xe6! Now 16...fxe6 17 ♕xe6+ and 16...♕e7 17 ♗d7+! are both decisive, but what about 16...♗e7 here? Black just about seems to be doing okay, e.g. 17 gxh5 ♖xh5!? 18 ♗g4 ♖e5 19 ♗e3 ♖d8 20 f4 ♖e4 or 17 ♗b3 0-0-0 18 g5 ♖he8.

14 g4 ♗g6 15 ♗c3 ♕c8

A depressing retreat, but after the

originally intended 15...♛c7 16 ♝xg7 ♛f4+ 17 ♔b1 ♜g8, White has the convincing *intermezzo* 18 ♜d4! (18 ♝e5? ♛e4! trades queens and relieves much of the pressure) 18...♛g5 19 ♝e5 (but not 19 f4? ♝xc2+!), when black's queen is in danger of being completely sealed out by f2-f4 or h2-h4.

16 ♝xg7 ♜g8 17 ♝e5 b5 18 ♝d3!

This is more accurate than 18 ♝b3, which allows Black chances of survival. Once these bishops are exchanged Black just has no way of defending the weaknesses. White already has a winning position.

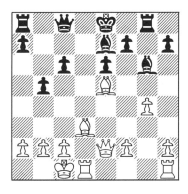

18...a5 19 f4 a4 20 ♜hf1 f6 21 ♝d4 ♝xd3 22 ♛xd3 c5

After 22...♜xg4 23 ♛xh7 or 22...♜g6 23 ♛h3 White's queen goes on a rampage.

23 ♛xh7 ♜f8 24 ♝e3 a3 25 b3 ♛c6 26 f5 c4

26...♛e4 loses to 27 ♝xc5!

27 fxe6 ♛xe6 28 ♜fe1 cxb3 29 ♝c5 1-0

see following diagram

Black cannot deal with the threats of ♜xe6 and ♛xe7+.

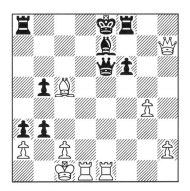

Game 10
Almasi-Kindermann
Austrian Team Championship 1995

1 e4 d5 2 exd5 ♛xd5 3 ♘c3 ♛a5 4 d4 c6 5 ♝c4 ♝f5 6 ♘f3 ♘f6 7 ♝d2 e6 8 ♘d5 ♛d8 9 ♘xf6+ gxf6!? 10 c3 ♛c7?!

Almasi considers 9...gxf6 to be dubious, but I suspect that this move is the real culprit. The idea behind 10...♛c7 is to seize control of the h2-b8 diagonal before White gets a chance to play ♝f4. Still, as far as I can see, this is not such a big deal. Black should probably be content with 10...♘d7 and if 11 ♝f4 there is always 11...♘b6 12 ♝e2 ♝d6 or 12...♘d5, both of which look okay.

11 ♘h4 ♝g6 12 ♛f3 ♘d7 13 ♛h3!

A powerful novelty which threatens 14 ♘xg6. Previously 13 ♝f4 had been played, but after 13...♝d6 14 ♝xd6 ♛xd6 15 ♛g3 ♛xg3 16 hxg3 0-0-0 17 0-0-0 c5 18 ♘xg6 hxg6 19 dxc5 ♘xc5 20 ♜xd8+ ♜xd8 21 ♜h7 ♜f8 22 f3 f5 23 ♔d2 ♔d8 24 ♜h4 ♔e7 25 ♝e2 e5 Black was at least equal in Van der Wiel-C.Hansen, Ter Apel

1993. Indeed, this turned out to be another smooth victory for the Danish number one.

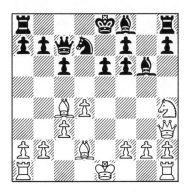

13...♝g7

Since 13...♖g8 fails to 14 ♗xe6!, Black is compelled to place the bishop on an inferior square. It can always be activated with ...f7-f5, but then the light-squared bishop will resemble a big pawn.

14 0-0 0-0-0 15 b4

Direct and energetic. White plans a pawn storm on the queenside. Meanwhile, due to Black's clogged up pieces, there is no similar threat on the other wing.

15...♚b8 16 a4 ♚a8 17 a5 f5 18 ♖fe1 ♞f6 19 ♗g5! ♖de8 20 ♗xf6 ♗xf6 21 ♞f3 ♛f4 22 ♞e5 ♗xe5 23 ♖xe5 ♛g4 24 ♛h6!

The position has simplified a little, but Black remains saddled with a shoddy bishop. Now White threatens the decisive ♗e2, which would snare the black queen.

24...♛h5 25 ♛e3 f6 26 ♖c5

26 ♖xe6 ♗f7 27 ♖xe8+ ♖xe8 28 ♛d3 is also winning, but the text is more to the point.

26...a6

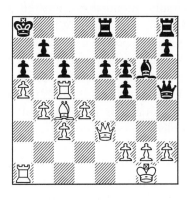

27 ♗xa6! bxa6 28 ♖xc6 f4 29 ♖xa6+ ♚b7 30 ♖b6+ ♚a8 31 ♖a6+ ♚b7 32 ♖b6+ ♚a8 33 ♛xf4 ♛d5 34 ♖a6+ ♚b7 35 ♖b6+ ♚a8 36 ♖a6+ ♚b7 37 ♖d6! ♛c4 38 a6+ ♚c8 39 a7 ♚b7 40 ♖d7+ 1-0

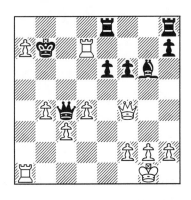

40...♚a8 41 ♛f3+ and 40...♚b6 41 ♛d6+ ♛c6 42 ♖a6+ are both winning. An excellent game from Almasi, but 10...♞d7 seems to be a major improvement for Black.

> *Game 11*
> **Szymanski-Grabowicz**
> *Correspondence 1993*

1 e4 d5 2 exd5 ♛xd5 3 ♞c3 ♛a5 4 d4 ♞f6 5 ♞f3 ♗f5 6 ♞e5

White's sharpest choice at this juncture.

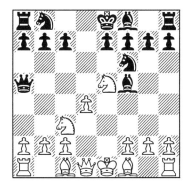

6...c6 7 g4

7 ♗c4 is considered in Games 12-15, but the restrained 7 ♗d3 is an additional option here, aiming for a small advantage. However, it is not particularly dangerous: after 7...♗xd3 8 ♕xd3 ♘bd7 9 ♘xd7 ♘xd7 10 0-0 e6 11 ♗f4 ♘f6 12 ♗e5 0-0-0 13 ♕f3 ♗e7 14 a3 ♕a6 Black had equalised in Thipsay-Van Wely, London 1992.

7 ♗f4 is rare, but certainly deserves attention. Michael Adams scored a very pretty win with this move at the Dublin Zonal in 1993. Adams-Ryan continued 7...e6 8 g4 ♗e4 9 ♘c4 ♕d8 10 ♘xe4 ♘xe4 11 ♕f3 ♘f6 12 0-0-0 h5 13 g5 ♕d5? 14 ♕b3! b5 15 gxf6 ♕xh1 16 fxg7 ♗xg7 17 ♕g3! ♗h6 18 ♗xh6 ♖xh6 19 ♘e5! ♕d5 20 ♕g8+ ♔e7 21 ♕xf7+ ♔d6 22 c4 and Black resigned.

7...♗e6 8 ♘c4

After 8 ♗c4? Black has the reply 8...♘xg4! 9 ♗xe6 ♘xe5, when in order to maintain the material balance White has to play the strange looking 10 ♗c8 ♕c7 11 ♗xb7 ♕xb7 12 dxe5. After 12...e6, however, White's dodgy kingside pawn structure gives Black an edge.

8...♕c7

There is no real justification for conceding the bishop pair. 8...♗xc4 9 ♗xc4 e6 10 ♕e2 ♗b4 11 ♗d2 ♘bd7 12 ♖g1 White had a small plus in Hector-C.Hansen, Kerteminde 1991.

9 h3

9 ♗e2? simply blunders a pawn to 9...♘xg4!

9...♘bd7 10 ♕f3 ♘d5 11 ♘e4 h6 12 ♗d2 g6 13 ♘a5 ♗g7 14 c4 ♘5f6 15 ♘g3 0-0

Despite being a little confined, Black has a perfectly playable position and after White's over-ambitious next move, there is much more to bite on.

16 0-0-0?! ♖ad8 17 ♘b3 b6 18 ♔b1 a5! 19 ♕e2 a4 20 ♘c1 ♖c8 21 ♗c3 b5!

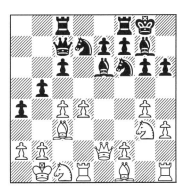

A typical idea, securing the outpost on d5 for the knight.

22 c5

After the greedy 22 cxb5 cxb5 23 ♕xb5 ♘d5 Black's compensation is overwhelming.

22...♘d5 23 ♗e1 a3 24 b3 ♘f4 25 ♕c2 ♗d5 26 ♖g1 e5!

Assuming total control. If the a1-h8

diagonal is opened, White's days will be numbered.

27 ♘d3 ♘e6 28 ♗c3 ♘xd4 29 ♗xd4 exd4 30 f4 ♖ce8 31 ♗g2 ♗xg2 32 ♕xg2 ♖e3 33 ♘e4 ♖e8 34 ♖ge1?

A blunder, but White was lost in any case.

34...♖8xe4 0-1

Game 12
Trindade-Soppe
Sao Paulo 1993

---

1 e4 d5 2 exd5 ♕xd5 3 ♘c3 ♕a5 4 d4 ♘f6 5 ♘f3 ♗f5 6 ♘e5 c6 7 ♗c4

Inaugurating a very menacing system.

7...e6 8 g4

The quiet 8 0-0 is considered in Games 14 and 15.

8...♗g6

For 8...♗e4?! see Game 13.

9 ♗d2

After 9 h4 we have a position similar to the line 5...♗g4 6 h3 ♗h5 7 g4 ♗g6 8 ♘e5 e6 9 ♗g2 c6 10 h4, the only difference being that the white bishop stands on c4 instead of g2, which ought to benefit Black. There are two ways forward:

a) 9...♗b4 10 ♗d2 ♘e4 11 f3! ♘xc3 12 bxc3 ♗xc3 13 ♖b1 b5 14 ♗b3 ♘d7?! (14...f6 is stronger, but 15 ♘xg6 hxg6 16 ♗xe6 still gives White an edge) 15 ♘xc6 ♗xd2+ 16 ♕xd2 ♕c7 17 d5 ♘f6 18 h5 ♘xd5 19 ♗xd5 exd5 was played in Campora-C.Hansen Palma de Mallorca 1989, when 20 ♘d4! would have given White a totally winning position.

b) 9...♘bd7! 10 ♘xd7 ♘xd7 11 h5

♗e4 12 ♖h3 ♗d5 13 ♗d3 0-0-0 14 ♗d2!? (now Black can snatch a pawn) 14...♕b6 15 ♘xd5 exd5 16 c3 ♕xb2 17 ♖f3 f6 18 ♖b1 ♕a3 19 c4 dxc4 20 ♗xc4 ♕e7+ 21 ♖e3 ♕d6 22 ♖e6 ♕xd4 23 ♗a6 ♘c5 24 ♖xc6+ ♔d7! and White's attack was repulsed in Rublevsky-Lastin, Elista 1995.

9...♕b6

Given the difficulties experienced after this move, perhaps Black should consider 9...♗b4!?, intending 10 a3 ♗xc3 11 ♗xc3 ♕c7 12 h4 ♗e4.

10 ♕e2!? ♘bd7

The b-pawn is poisoned. 10...♕xb2? 11 ♖b1 ♕xc2 12 ♖xb7 ♗e7 allows 13 ♘xf7!, when 13...♗xf7 14 ♗d3 traps the queen and 13...♔xf7 14 ♕xe6+ ♔f8 15 ♕xe7 is mate. Grabbing the d-pawn is a better bet, but White obviously still has reasonable compensation after 10...♕xd4!? 11 0-0-0.

11 f4 0-0-0

Now 11...♕xd4 loses to 12 ♘f3 ♕b6 13 f5.

12 0-0-0 ♘xe5 13 dxe5 ♘d5

14 ♖hf1!

This rook will be able to swing to the queenside via f3, giving White an irresistible attack.

14...h6 15 f5 ♗h7 16 ♖f3 ♗e7 17 ♘xd5 cxd5 18 ♖b3! ♕d4 19 ♗a6! ♖d7

Or 19...bxa6 20 ♕xa6+ ♔d7 21 ♕b5+ ♔c7 22 ♕b7 mate.

20 ♗xb7+ 1-0

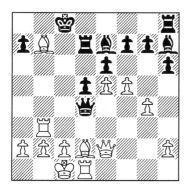

Czech GM Blatny gives the following finish: 20...♖xb7 21 ♕a6 ♕b6 22 ♖xb6 axb6 23 ♕a8+ ♖b8 24 ♕c6+ ♔d8 25 ♗e3 ♗g5 26 ♗xg5+ hxg5 27 ♕d6+ ♔c8 28 ♖d3.

> ## Game 13
> ## Aseev-König
> ## *Munich 1990*

1 e4 d5 2 exd5 ♕xd5 3 ♘c3 ♕a5 4 d4 ♘f6 5 ♘f3 ♗f5 6 ♘e5 c6 7 ♗c4 e6 8 g4 ♗e4?!

This over-ambitious move has received some severe punishment.

9 0-0 ♗d5 10 ♗d3 ♗d6 11 f4 c5 12 g5! cxd4 13 ♘b5 ♗c5

Black is forced into this speculative line, as 13...♘e4 runs into 14 ♖e1 ♗b4 15 ♖xe4! ♗xe4 16 ♘c4 ♕xb5 17 ♘d6+ ♗xd6 18 ♗xb5+.

14 f5!

Excellent play by Aseev. After the immediate 14 gxf6 gxf6 Black acquires some undeserved counterplay on the g-file.

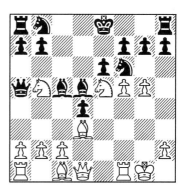

14...♘c6 15 ♗f4! ♘xe5 16 ♗xe5 0-0-0 17 fxe6! ♗c6

Aseev criticises this, but after the alternative 17...fxe6 18 gxf6 gxf6 19 ♖xf6 ♖hg8+ 20 ♗g3 White is simply a piece up.

18 exf7 ♖d5 19 gxf6 g6

Or 19...♖xe5 20 ♕g4+ ♗d7 21 fxg7!

20 ♕e1?!

This is unnecessarily pretentious. 20 ♕g4+ ♗d7 21 ♕e4 ♗c6 22 ♗g3 is a clean kill.

20...♗b4 21 ♘xa7+! ♔d7 22 ♘xc6 bxc6 23 ♗g3!?

23 c3 also wins after 23...♖xe5 24 cxb4 ♕d5 25 ♕h4 ♖g5+ 26 ♔f2 ♕g2+ 27 ♔e1, as Black has run out of checks.

23...♗xe1 24 ♖axe1 h5 25 ♖e7+ ♔c8 26 b4 ♕xa2

26...♕xb4 27 ♗a6+ ♔d8 28 ♗c7 is a pleasant checkmate.

27 ♖c7+ ♔d8 28 ♖b7

Finally the tie is settled. The threat of ♖b8+ forces Black to return the queen, handing White a winning endgame.

28...♕a8 29 ♖b8+ ♕xb8 30 ♗xb8 ♖f8 31 ♗c4 ♖g5+ 32 ♔h1 c5 33 ♗d6 1-0

1 e4 d5 2 exd5 ♕xd5 3 ♘c3 ♕a5 4 d4 c6 5 ♘f3 ♘f6 6 ♘e5 ♗f5 7 ♗c4 e6 8 0-0 ♘bd7 9 ♘xd7

This peaceful system is not particularly popular and should not pose too many problems for Black. 9 ♖e1 is discussed in the next game.

9...♘xd7 10 ♗f4

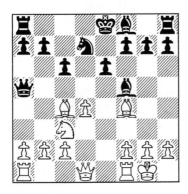

10...♗e7!

The most accurate response to White's play. 10...♗b4 has also been played here, but given that ♘c3-e2-g3 is White's plan, it is foolish to give him an extra tempo with a later c2-c3.

11 ♘e2 0-0 12 ♘g3 ♗g6 13 ♖e1

After this move Black obtains awkward pressure against White's d4-pawn. 13 c3 suggests itself, intending to meet 13...♘b6 14 ♗b3 ♖fd8 with 15 ♕e2.

13...♘b6 14 ♗b3 ♖fd8!

Black already has the more com-

fortable position.

15 ♗d2 ♕a6 16 ♕g4 c5 17 c3 ♘c4 18 ♗xc4 ♕xc4 19 ♗e3 ♗f6 20 h4 cxd4 21 cxd4 h6 22 h5 ♗h7 23 ♖ed1

The immediate 23 ♗xh6 loses a piece to 23...♖xd4.

23...♔f8 24 b3 ♕d5

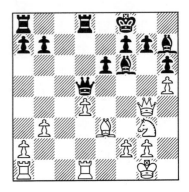

Let us take stock of the position. Black has the two bishops and White has a weak isolated d-pawn, which is firmly blockaded. Realising the unhappy state of his position, Cladouras goes into 'swindle mode'.

25 ♖ac1 ♖ac8 26 ♖xc8 ♖xc8 27 ♖d2 ♗e7 28 ♖d1 ♖c2 29 ♕f4 ♗d6 30 ♕h4 ♗c7 31 ♖c1 ♖xc1+ 32 ♗xc1 ♕a5 33 ♗f4 ♗d8 34 ♗d6+ ♔e8 35 ♕g4 ♗f6

All the 'one movers' have been dealt with and White's position is in ruins. In fact, a pawn has to drop due to the dual threats on d4 and a2.

36 ♗e5 ♕e1+ 37 ♔h2 ♕xf2 38 ♗xf6 ♕xf6 39 d5? exd5 40 ♕c8+ ♕d8 41 ♕g4 ♔f8 42 ♘e2 ♗e4 43 ♘d4 ♔g8 44 ♕f4 a6 0-1

A very smooth positional effort. Notice that Black was very comfortably placed in this isolated queen's pawn (IQP) position, especially with his light-squared bishop posted actively outside the pawn chain.

Game 15
M.Pribyl-N.Michaelsen
German Bundesliga 1994
---

1 e4 d5 2 exd5 ♕xd5 3 ♘c3 ♕a5 4 d4 ♘f6 5 ♘f3 ♗f5 6 ♘e5

Another placid system is 6 ♗d3, after which Black again can look forward to the future with some confidence, e.g. 6...♘bd7 7 0-0 e6 8 ♗f4 c6 9 ♘e5 ♘xe5 10 ♗xe5 ♗g6 11 a3 ♗e7 12 b4 ♕d8 13 ♕e2 ♗xd3 14 ♕xd3 0-0 15 ♖fd1 ♘d5 16 ♘e2 b5! as in Maus-C.Hansen, Hamburg 1991.

6...c6 7 ♗c4 e6 8 0-0 ♘bd7 9 ♖e1

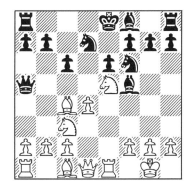

9...♘xe5!

Of course the standard 9...♗b4 is possible here, but 9...♘xe5 gives White a bit of an early headache.

10 dxe5

10 ♖xe5 ♕c7 gains time because of the annoying threat of ...♗d6. Note that 11 ♕e2 is met by 11...♘g4! when 12 ♖xf5 ♕xh2+ 13 ♔f1 ♕h1 is mate.

10...♘g4 11 ♕e2

After 11 ♗f4 Black has:

a) 11...♘xf2 12 ♕f3! ♗c5 13 ♔f1 and Black's offside knight gave White compensation for the pawn in Antonio-Westerinen, Manila 1992.

b) I prefer 11...♗c5!, when both 12 ♘e4 and 12 ♗g3 can still be answered by 12...♘xf2!, as Black always regains the piece with ...♕c5+.

11...♗c5 12 ♘d1

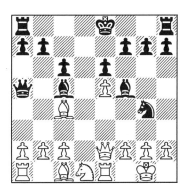

12...♗xc2!

A surprising trick which leaves White in absolute disarray. Now 13 ♕xc2 ♕xe1 is mate, so...

13 ♗d2 ♕d8! 14 ♕xg4

The tactics favour Black after 14 ♗f4 ♗xd1! 15 ♖axd1 ♗xf2+ 16 ♕xf2 (or 16 ♔h1 ♕h4) 16...♘xf2 17 ♖xd8+ ♖xd8 18 ♔xf2 and now 18...♖d4!, attacking both bishops.

14...♕xd2 15 ♘e3 ♗g6 16 h4 0-0 17 h5 ♗f5 18 ♕f3 ♗xe3 19 ♖xe3 ♕xb2

The smoke has lifted, leaving Black with a totally winning position.

20 ♖ae1 ♕d4 21 ♗e2 ♖fd8 22 g4 ♗c2 23 h6 ♖d5 24 hxg7 ♖xe5 25 ♕f6 ♖d5 26 ♗f3? ♕xf6 27 ♗xd5 cxd5 0-1

So it seems that 9 ♖e1 is nothing for Black to worry about.

Summary

Of all of White's options in this chapter, the one which gives Black the most to worry about is the adventurous 6 ♘e5 c6 7 ♗c4 e6 8 g4. An improvement is required in Game 12, which by all accounts was something of a battering for Black. If White opts to play quietly, however, Black can usually reach a comfortable position and can often seize the initiative as well.

1 e4 d5 2 exd5 ♕xd5 3 ♘c3 ♕a5 4 d4 ♘f6 5 ♘f3 ♗f5

6 ♗d2 *(D)*

    6 ♘e5 c6

        7 g4 - *game 11*

        7 ♗c4 e6

            8 g4 *(D)*

                8...♗g6 - *game 12*

                8...♗e4 - *game 13*

            8 0-0 ♘bd7

                9 ♘xd7 - *game 14*

                9 ♖e1 - *game 15*

6...c6 7 ♗c4 e6 8 ♘d5 ♕d8 9 ♘xf6+ *(D)*

    9...♕xf6 - *game 9*

    9...gxf6 - *game 10*

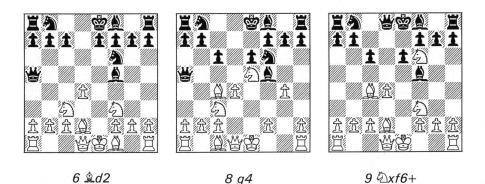

     6 ♗d2   *8 g4*   *9 ♘xf6+*

CHAPTER THREE

2...♛xd5: Fifth Move Alternatives

1 e4 d5 2 exd5 ♛xd5 3 ♘c3 ♛a5 4 d4 ♘f6

Here we examine deviations for both White and Black on the fifth move, the most important of which is 5...♝g4 (Games 16-19), which was utilised by the Australian Grandmaster Ian Rogers with some success in the 1980s. This used to be considered the principal line of the 2...♛xd5 variation. Unfortunately, towards the end of the 1980s it took a bit of a hammering, with White players finding numerous ways to virtually refute Black's opening plan. At first Rogers was able to resuscitate some of the variations, but eventually even he was forced to concede defeat and drop this line from his repertoire. Still, opening fashion is a fickle thing, so there is always a possibility that 5...♝g4 could be revived in the dim and distant future.

5...♘c6 has an even poorer reputation than 5...♝g4. I suppose it does have the advantage of being very complex, but well prepared White players should be able to emerge with a definite advantage, as we shall see in Games 20 and 21.

5...c6 (Games 22 and 23) is a differ-

ent story altogether, and has the advantage of flexibility. Even the PCA World Champion Garry Kasparov could not come up with anything useful against it in Game 22. Indeed, he obtained a distinctly inferior position after only fifteen moves, which can only be an excellent advert for the Scandinavian!

Most of White's fifth move alternatives are not particularly important, as generally Black has the option of steering back into the main lines. However 5 ♝c4!? (Game 24) is interesting, as there can be certain benefits in delaying the development of the king's knight.

> ### Game 16
> ### Popovic-Rogers
> *Vrsac 1987*

1 e4 d5 2 exd5 ♛xd5 3 ♘c3 ♛a5 4 d4 ♘f6 5 ♘f3 ♝g4 6 h3 ♝h5 7 g4!

The most testing move. For 7 ♝d2 see Game 19.

7...♝g6 8 ♘e5

The speculative 8 b4!? has also been witnessed here. Following 8...♛xb4 (apart from being rather cowardly, there is also absolutely nothing wrong with 8...♕b6!?) 9 ♗d2 ♕d6 10 ♖b1 there have been a couple of tussles:

a) 10...b6 11 ♗g2 c6 12 ♘e5! gave White a very dangerous initiative in Volkov-Nenov, Shumen 1990.

b) 10...♘d5!?, returning the pawn, may be the antidote. A postal game from 1991 between Temmink and Smit proceeded with 11 ♖xb7 ♘xc3 12 ♗xc3 ♗e4 13 ♖b2 ♘d7 14 ♗b5 c6 15 ♗d3 ♗d5 16 ♗e2 h5 17 g5 ♘b6 18 ♗b4 ♕e6 19 ♕d3 ♘c4 20 ♖b1 g6 21 ♗c5 ♗g7 22 ♖b4 ♘d6 23 c4 ♗e4 24 ♕e3 ♘f5 25 ♕f4 0-0 26 0-0 ♖fd8, when Black had weathered the storm successfully, leaving the white position looking rather disorganised.

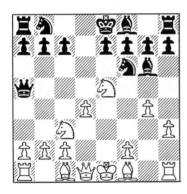

8...e6 9 ♗g2

The immediate 9 h4 is considered, along with 9 ♘c4, in Game 18.

9...c6 10 h4 ♗e4

10...♘bd7 is discussed in the next game, while 10...♗b4 11 ♗d2 is dealt with (by transposition) in the notes to Game 18.

11 ♗xe4 ♘xe4 12 ♕f3 ♘d6 13 ♗f4!

This is more effective than 13 ♗d2 f6 14 ♘d3 ♘d7 15 ♕e2 0-0-0 16 f4 h5 17 0-0-0, when the players agreed a

draw in Chandler-Rogers, Nis 1983.

13...f6

After 13...♘b5!? White can contemplate 14 ♘xf7!? ♘xd4 15 ♕e4 ♘xc2+ 16 ♕xc2 ♔xf7 17 0-0-0 with obvious compensation for the pawn deficit, while 13...♘a6? is just a straightforward blunder, allowing 14 ♘xc6! as in Gufeld-Korolev, Russia 1985.

14 ♘d3 ♘b5?!

Failing to foresee White's next move. In his notes to the game Rogers gives 14...♘d7 15 0-0-0 0-0-0 16 ♖he1 ♖e8 as only slightly better for White.

15 0-0! ♘xd4?!

Rogers suggests that 15...♘xc3 might have been a better try, although after 16 bxc3 ♕xc3 17 ♕e4 ♕c4 18 ♖ab1 Black's position is not particularly inspiring.

16 ♕e4 ♕d8

16...e5 loses to 17 ♘xe5 fxe5 18 ♗xe5 ♘e6 19 ♗xb8.

17 ♖ad1 ♕d7 18 ♗e3! c5 19 ♘xc5

19...♗xc5 20 ♗xd4 ♗xd4 21 ♖xd4 ♕c6 22 ♖fd1! 0-0

The position has simplified somewhat, but White still remains in total control. On 22...♕xe4 comes 23

♖xe4! ♔f7 (23...e5 24 ♘b5 ♘a6 25 ♘d6+ ♔e7 26 ♘f5+) 24 ♘b5 ♘a6 25 ♘d6+ ♔e7 26 ♘f5+ and White wins. **23 ♖d6 ♕xe4 24 ♘xe4 e5 25 ♘c5 ♘c6! 26 ♘xb7 ♘d4 27 c3 ♘f3+ 28 ♔f1!? ♘h2+ 29 ♔e2 ♘xg4 30 ♘d8!**

Paving the way for White's queenside pawns, which will eventually decide the game.

30...h5 31 ♘e6 ♖f7 32 c4! ♖e7 33 c5 ♔f7 34 ♘d8+ ♔e8 35 b4! e4 36 ♘c6 ♖c7 37 b5 f5 38 a4 ♖ac8 39 ♖d8+ ♖xd8 40 ♖xd8+ ♔f7 41 ♖d6!

1-0

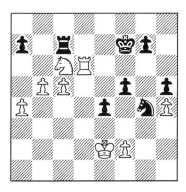

There is no real answer to b5-b6. A powerful performance from Popovic, which seems to be a complete answer to 10...♗e4.

Game 17
Smirin-Asanov
Beijing Open 1991

---

1 e4 d5 2 exd5 ♕xd5 3 ♘c3 ♕a5 4 d4 ♘f6 5 ♘f3 ♗g4 6 h3 ♗h5 7 g4 ♗g6 8 ♘e5 e6 9 ♗g2 c6 10 h4 ♘bd7!?

This is certainly a more testing alternative to 10...♗e4. Although Black's position sometimes hangs by a

very small thread, no outright refutation has yet been discovered.

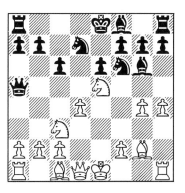

11 ♘xd7 ♔xd7 12 ♗d2

Karpov's suggestion of 12 d5!? is critical here. Black is obliged to play 12...exd5, as 12...cxd5 13 h5 ♗e4 14 f3 and 12...♘xd5 13 h5 both win for White. After 12...exd5 13 h5 ♗e4? 14 f3 ♗b4 15 ♗d2 ♕c7 16 fxe4 ♕g3+ 17 ♔f1 ♔d8? 18 ♘e2 Black was forced to resign in Rogers-Zeidler, Melbourne 1990 (a rare appearance on the white side by the Australian GM). However, 13...♖e8+ is certainly a stronger move. After 14 ♔f1 ♕a6+ 15 ♔g1 (15 ♘e2 ♖xe2! 16 ♕xe2 ♕xe2+ 17 ♔xe2 ♗xc2 is fine for Black) 15...♗e4 16 f3 ♗c5+ 17 ♔h2 ♗d6+ 18 ♔h3 ♗g6!? we reach an unusual position. Black is a pawn up, but the bishop is trapped and it is just a case of whether Black can secure enough compensation before White rounds it up. Objectively White is better, but Black obviously has some practical chances.

12...h5?

Not the best move. The Argentinean IM Soppe has achieved some success with 12...h6. Here are a couple of his encounters:

a) 13 ♘d5 ♕a4 14 b3 ♕xd4 15 ♘xf6+ gxf6 16 ♗xh6 ♗d3! 17 ♕xd3 (17 ♗xf8 ♕c3+) 17...♕xd3 18 cxd3 ♗xh6 19 ♔e2 ♖hg8 and Black had no problems in Zapata-Soppe, Havana (Capablanca Memorial) 1991.

b) 13 d5 exd5 14 h5 ♗h7 15 ♘xd5 ♖e8+ 16 ♘e3 ♕a4 17 0-0 ♗d6 18 c4 ♕xd1 19 ♖axd1 ♔c7 20 ♗c3 ♗e5 21 ♗xe5+ ♖xe5 22 ♖d4 ♖d8 and again Black was equal in Malbran-Soppe, Buenos Aires 1991.

13 g5 ♘g8 14 d5!

Now this advance packs even more punch.

14...exd5 15 ♘xd5 ♖e8+ 16 ♘e3 ♕a4 17 b3 ♕f4 18 ♔f1! ♔c8 19 ♗h3+ ♔b8 20 ♘d5

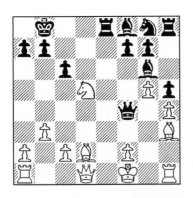

The winning move. Black cannot avoid material losses.

20...♕d6 21 ♗f4 ♖e5 22 ♗xe5 ♕xe5 23 ♘f6! ♕d6 24 ♘d7+ ♔a8 1-0

Black resigned without waiting for 25 ♕xd6 ♗xd6 26 ♖d1 ♗e7 27 ♘e5. It seems that Black's hopes lie with 12...h6 in this line.

> ### Game 18
> ### Hardicsay-Feistenauer
> *Dornbirn 1987*

1 e4 d5 2 exd5 ♕xd5 3 ♘c3 ♕a5 4 d4 ♘f6 5 ♘f3 ♗g4 6 h3 ♗h5 7 g4 ♗g6 8 ♘e5 e6 9 h4

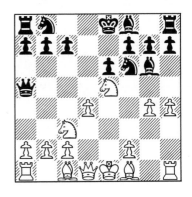

9 h4 is another reliable way to obtain an advantage against 5...♗g4. Aside from this there is also 9 ♘c4, which forces the black queen to an awkward square. Pinkas-Bellon Lopez, Bern Open 1992, saw 9...♕a6 10 h4 ♗b4 11 h5 ♕c6 12 ♖h3 ♗e4 13 ♘d2! ♘bd7 14 a3 ♗xc3 15 ♖xc3 ♕b6 16 g5 ♘d5 17 ♘xe4 ♘xc3 18 bxc3, when White had already reached a winning position.

9...♗b4 10 ♗d2!

Following an impressive win by

Karpov against Ian Rogers in this line, 10 ♖h3 had become the most popular move here. However, Rogers then managed to improve on Black's defence in the game Lobron-Rogers, Biel 1984, which saw 10...♗xc3+ 11 bxc3 ♘bd7 12 ♘xg6 hxg6 13 ♖b1 0-0-0 14 ♖b5 ♕a4, and Black was doing okay, albeit in a very messy position.

10...♕b6 11 ♗g2 c6?

This position could also arise from the move order 9 ♗g2 c6 10 h4 ♗b4 11 ♗d2 ♕b6. A big improvement for Black is 11...♗xc3!, which has the merit of retaining the piece. After 12 ♗xc3 ♗e4 13 ♗xe4 ♘xe4 14 ♕f3 ♘d6 15 0-0-0 ♘c6 16 d5 ♘xe5 17 ♗xe5 0-0 18 h5 ♘c4 19 ♗xg7! e5! (19...♔xg7 20 ♕c3+) 20 ♕b3 ♘xb2 21 ♗xf8 ♕xb3 22 axb3 ♘xd1 23 ♖xd1 ♔xf8 24 ♔d2 a5 Black was only slightly worse in the endgame in Steinfl-Rogers, Lugano Open 1989.

12 h5! ♕xd4

12...♗xc3!? is stronger, although White keeps an advantage after 13 bxc3 ♗e4 14 f3.

13 ♘f3 ♕xg4 14 hxg6

14...♕xg6

Black can recover the piece with

14...♕xg2, but after 15 gxf7+ ♔f8 16 ♖g1 ♕h3 17 ♕e2, intending 0-0-0, his days are numbered. After 14...♕xg6 Black has three pawns for the bishop, but still suffers from a lack of development. Furthermore, the position has opened up perfectly for White's active pieces.

15 ♗f1! ♗xc3 16 ♗xc3 ♘d5 17 ♕d4 ♘xc3 18 ♕xc3 ♕e4+ 19 ♗e2 f6 20 ♖h4! ♕d5 21 ♖d4 ♕f5 22 0-0-0 0-0 23 ♗d3! 1-0

After 23...♕h5 24 ♖h4 the h-pawn goes, as does the rest of Black's position.

> ### Game 19
> **Miles-Hickl**
> *Zagreb 1987*

1 e4 d5 2 exd5 ♕xd5 3 ♘c3 ♕a5 4 d4 ♘f6 5 ♘f3 ♗g4 6 h3 ♗h5

Naturally Black can also play 6...♗xf3 here, which is a reasonably solid, but hardly complete answer to Black's problems. After 7 ♕xf3 c6 8 ♗d2 ♘bd7 9 0-0-0 e6 10 ♔b1 White clearly retains a comfortable edge.

7 ♗d2

A poor relation to 7 g4!

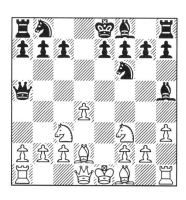

7...e6 8 ♗c4 ♗b4!

This is more convincing than 8...c6, which allows White to retain the advantage with 9 ♘d5! After 9...♕d8 10 ♘xf6+ ♕xf6? (10...gxf6 11 c3 is only slightly better for White) 11 g4 ♗g6 12 ♕e2! (12 ♗g5 ♗xc2 13 ♕e2 ♕g6 was Black's idea, but 12 ♕e2 is much stronger) 12...♗xc2 13 ♖c1! ♕g6 (13...♗g6 14 ♗g5) 14 ♗f4! ♗b4+ 15 ♔f1 ♗b1 (again the only move, as 15...♗e4 fails to 16 ♘e5) 16 ♖xb1! ♕xb1+ 17 ♔g2 ♕g6 18 ♗d3 f5 19 ♗xf5 White has an overwhelming position. Chandler-Rogers, Hong Kong 1984, concluded 19...♕f6 20 ♗g5 ♕f7 21 ♗xe6 ♕c7 22 ♗b3+ ♔f8 23 ♘e5 ♗e7 24 ♖e1 ♔e8 25 ♘f7 ♖f8 and Black resigned before White could play 26 ♕xe7+ ♕xe7 27 ♖xe7 mate.

9 g4 ♗g6 10 ♘e5 ♘c6! 11 ♘xc6

In his notes Hickl gives two other possibilities for White:

a) 11 ♘xg6 hxg6 12 a3 ♗xc3 13 ♗xc3 ♕g5 with an edge for Black.

b) 11 a3 ♘xe5!? 12 axb4 ♘f3+! 13 ♕xf3 ♕xa1+ 14 ♔e2 ♕xb2 15 ♖b1 ♕xc2 16 ♗b3 ♕xb1 17 ♘xb1 ♗xb1 and the material imbalance favours Black.

11...bxc6 12 a3 ♗xc3 13 ♗xc3 ♕b6

13...♕g5!, preparing ...h7-h5, would have been even more effective. It seems that the plan of g2-g4, combined with ♗c4, asks too much of the white position. Certainly the bishop would now prefer to be on g2!

14 b3 ♘e4 15 ♗b2 h5 16 f3 ♘d6 17 ♗d3 ♗xd3 18 ♕xd3 hxg4 19 fxg4 ♕a5+ 20 ♕d2 ♕xd2+ 21 ♔xd2

0-0-0 22 ♔e3

We have reached an endgame in which Black has no problems. His queenside pawns are split, but White's h3-pawn is also a major weakness.

22...♖h7 23 ♔f3 ♖dh8 24 ♔g2 f5 25 ♖af1 ♖h4 26 d5 cxd5 27 ♗xg7 ♖g8 28 ♔g3 ♖h7 29 ♗e5 ♘e4+ 30 ♔f4 ♖g5 31 ♗f6 ♖g6

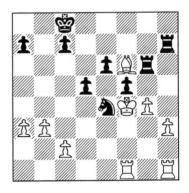

32 ♗a1?

The losing move. White had to keep the pressure on c7 with 32 ♗e5. Then 32...♖h4 33 ♖fg1 fxg4 34 hxg4 ♖gxg4+ 35 ♖xg4 ♖xh1 36 ♖g7 c5 should end in a draw.

32...♖h4 33 ♖hg1 ♘g5! 34 ♗f6 ♘xh3+ 35 ♔e5 ♖hxg4 36 ♖xg4 fxg4 37 ♗h4 g3 38 ♗xg3 ♖xg3 39 ♔xe6 c6 40 ♔d6 ♖c3 41 ♖f7 ♖xc2 42 ♖xa7 d4 43 ♖c7+ ♔b8 44 ♖h7 ♘f4 45 ♖h4 ♘e2 46 ♖h8+ ♔b7 47 ♖h7+ ♔b6 48 ♖h8 ♘c3 49 ♖b8+ ♔a7 50 ♔c7 ♘b5+ 51 ♔c8 ♘xa3 52 b4 d3 53 ♖b7+ ♔a6 54 ♔c7 ♘b5+ 0-1

Game 20
Perfilev-Reprintsev
Correspondence 1990

1 e4 d5 2 exd5 ♕xd5 3 ♘c3 ♕a5 4

d4 ♘f6 5 ♘f3 ♘c6

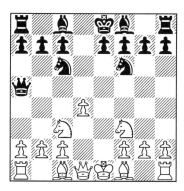

A provocative move. Black's goal is rapid queenside development and instant pressure on White's d4-pawn. Often Black will castle queenside in an attempt to disrupt White's smooth development plans. On the negative side, ...c7-c6 is no longer an option, so the queen is often lacking useful retreat squares. White can use this fact by immediately hassling the lady.

6 ♗d2!

Together with 6 ♗b5 (Game 21), this represents White's only chance of maintaining an advantage. Others fail to impress:

a) 6 d5 ♘b4 7 ♗b5+ ♗d7 transposes to 6 ♗b5 ♗d7 7 d5 ♘b4 (see the next game).

b) 6 ♗c4?! ♗g4 7 0-0 0-0-0. Black's objective has been achieved and he already stands better.

c) 6 ♗e2 ♗g4 7 ♗e3 0-0-0 8 ♘d2 ♗xe2 9 ♕xe2 ♕f5 10 ♘b3 e5! and Black has equalised comfortably.

6...♗g4

6...a6 has the benefit of preventing 7 ♘b5, but it really is just a little too extravagant. The miniature Ernst-Envik, Gausdal 1995, concluded 7

♗c4 ♕h5 8 ♘e5 ♘xe5 9 ♕xh5 ♘d3+ 10 cxd3 ♘xh5 11 ♘d5 ♔d8 12 ♖c1 g6 13 ♗b3 ♗f5 14 ♘xc7 1-0. Enough said!

7 ♘b5 ♕b6 8 c4!

This is certainly the safest move, but in my opinion it is also the best one. The elementary threat of c4-c5 forces a tactical sequence which leads to a very agreeable endgame for White. In contrast after 8 a4!? Black has every chance to muddy the waters. That said, it does come very close to being a forced win for White! After 8...♗xf3 9 ♕xf3? a6 there are two branches:

a) 10 d5 ♘e5 11 ♕g3 ♘e4 12 ♕f4 ♘xd2 13 ♕xe5 axb5 14 ♔xd2 bxa4 with advantage to Black in Lecuyer-Prie, French Team Championship 1993.

b) 10 a5 axb5 11 axb6 ♖xa1+ and now:

b1) 12 ♔e2 ♘xd4+ 13 ♔e3 ♘xf3 14 ♗xb5+ c6 15 ♗xc6+ bxc6 16 b7 ♖a3+!! 17 bxa3 ♘d7 18 ♔xf3 e5 wins for Black.

b2) 12 ♗c1 ♖xc1+ 13 ♔d2 ♖xc2+ 14 ♔d1 ♖xb2 15 ♕a3 ♖b1+ 16 ♔c2 ♖xf1! 17 ♕a8+ ♔d7 18 ♕xb7 ♘d5 and Black was better in Lafora-De Veer, Correspondence 1926.

So after 8 a4 ♗xf3 White should play 9 gxf3!, keeping the awesome threat of c4-c5. After 9...a5 10 ♗e3! ♘d5 11 c4 ♘xe3 12 fxe3 Black is in trouble. 12...♘a7 loses to 13 c5 ♕c6 14 ♘xa7 and 12...♘b4 runs into 13 c5 ♕c6 14 ♘d6+! and 15 ♗b5. This leaves 9...♘xd4 as Black's best chance. As far as I can see, the consequences of the variation 10 ♗e3 e5 (or

10...c5!?) 11 c3 a6 12 cxd4 axb5 13 ♗xb5+ c6 14 dxe5 ♕a5+ 15 ♗d2 ♗b4 are not clear at all. In the context of other assessments in this line, that can only be described as good news for Black.

8...♗xf3 9 ♕xf3 ♘xd4 10 ♘xd4 ♕xd4 11 ♕xb7 ♕e4+ 12 ♕xe4 ♘xe4 13 ♗e3

We have reached a very pleasant endgame for White, who has the better pawn structure and the two bishops.

13...e6

13...e5 doesn't change the assessment of the position. After 14 ♗d3 ♘c5 15 0-0-0 ♗d6 16 ♗c2 ♘e6 17 ♗a4+ ♔e7 18 ♗c6 ♖ad8 19 ♖d5 ♘d4 20 ♗xd4 exd4 21 ♖e1+ ♔f6 22 ♖e4 g5 23 g3 ♗b4 24 ♖exd4 Black was still suffering in Yemelin-Al.Ivanov, St Petersburg Open 1993.

14 g3 ♖b8 15 ♗g2 ♘c5 16 ♗c6+ ♔d8 17 0-0-0+ ♔c8 18 a3 ♖b6 19 ♗e8! ♘b3+ 20 ♔c2 ♗c5 21 ♗d7+ ♔b7 22 ♗xc5 ♘xc5 23 b4 ♘xd7 24 ♖xd7

Black has succeeded in exchanging off White's bishop pair, but has been forced to concede 'seventh heaven'.

The rest is quite straightforward.

24...♖d6 25 ♖xf7 ♖hd8 26 ♖c1 ♖d2+ 27 ♔b3 g5 28 ♖c2 ♖8d3+ 29 ♖c3 h5 30 b5 a6 31 a4 axb5 32 axb5 ♔b6 33 ♖f6 ♖xc3+ 34 ♔xc3 ♖e2 35 ♔d3 ♖e5 36 f4 gxf4 37 gxf4 ♖e1 38 f5 ♖d1+ 39 ♔e2 ♖h1 40 fxe6 1-0

1 e4 d5 2 exd5 ♕xd5 3 ♘c3 ♕a5 4 d4 ♘f6 5 ♘f3 ♘c6 6 ♗b5

Although 6 ♗b5 is a very natural looking move, White finds it surprisingly difficult to maintain an advantage with it.

6...♗d7 7 0-0!?

7 d5!? is a critical response to Black's play, but after 7...♘b4 8 ♗xd7+ ♘xd7 9 a3 ♘f6 10 axb4 ♕xa1 11 0-0 ♕a6! (an improvement over 11...♖d8) 12 ♘e5 g6 13 ♘d3 ♕c4 14 ♗e3 ♗g7 15 ♕f3 0-0 White had some compensation for the exchange, but probably not enough in Hunerkopf-Badzarani, Yalta 1989.

7...0-0-0 8 ♗e3

I reckon 8 ♕e2 gives White more hope of an edge. The game Belikov-Maliutin, Sochi 1990, continued 8...a6 9 ♗xc6 ♗xc6 10 ♘e5 ♗e8 11 ♗e3 ♘d5 12 ♘xd5 ♕xd5 13 c4 ♕e6. Here Belikov played 14 f4?!, allowing 14...f6! 15 d5 ♕f5 16 ♘f3 ♗h5 17 ♕f2 ♗xf3 18 ♕xf3 e6 19 dxe6 ♖d3!, and Black had more than equalised. Instead of 14 f4, I prefer the prophylactic 14 ♘f3! This prepares to answer 14...f6 and 14...g6 with 15 d5, in each case with a pull for White.

8...♘d5 9 ♕e2 ♘xc3 10 bxc3 a6 11 a4?! f6 12 d5 ♘b8 13 ♘d4

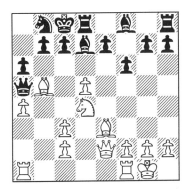

13...♕xc3

Black grabs a safe pawn. In fact it is not at all clear why Black cannot simply snatch the piece as well with 13...axb5 14 axb5 ♕xc3.

14 ♗c4 g6 15 ♖ab1 e5! 16 dxe6 ♗xa4 17 ♖a1 ♗e8 18 ♖fb1

Dropping two pieces for a rook, but after the alternative 18 ♖fd1 Black keeps the advantage with 18...♗c5. For example, 19 ♘f5 ♖xd1+ 20 ♖xd1 gxf5 21 ♗xc5 b5! 22 ♗d4 ♕xc4 23 ♕xc4 bxc4 24 ♗xf6 ♗h5 and Black wins.

18...♖xd4 19 ♗xd4 ♕xd4 20 e7

♗xe7 21 ♕xe7 ♕xc4 22 ♕xf6 ♖g8 23 ♖d1 ♗d7 24 ♖e1 ♘c6 25 ♖ad1 ♖d8 26 ♕g7 ♕xc2 27 ♕xh7 ♕f5 28 ♖e3 ♕h5 29 ♕xh5 gxh5 30 h4 a5 31 ♖d5 ♗e8 32 ♖g5 a4 33 ♖g8 ♗f7 34 ♖g7 ♗c4 35 g4 b5 0-1

The queenside pawns will land after 36 gxh5 b4 37 h6 b3 38 h7 b2 39 ♖e1 a3. A rather messy game which seems to reinforce the view that 6 ♗d2! is the best answer to 5...♘c6.

Game 22
Kasparov-Anand
PCA World Ch., New York 1995

1 e4 d5 2 exd5 ♕xd5 3 ♘c3 ♕a5 4 d4 ♘f6 5 ♘f3 c6

If Black intends to play the main line, 5...c6 is perhaps the most flexible choice here. Its biggest plus, as shown in this game, is that Black has the option of answering 6 ♘e5 with 6...♗e6 instead of 6...♗f5.

6 ♘e5 ♗e6

This looks like an unusual square for the bishop, but in fact it has many uses here. 6...♗e6 takes the sting out of ♘c4 and ♗c4 ideas and also prepares a kingside fianchetto. It is significant that the bishop cannot be pestered by ♘f3-g5, as the knight has already committed itself to e5.

7 ♗d3

7 ♗c4 is seen in the next game.

7...♘bd7

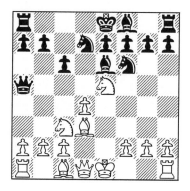

8 f4?!

After the game Kasparov criticised his play in the opening, saying that he hadn't been able to decide between aggression and restraint. It certainly seems that 8 f4 is a little too optimistic, as Anand now comfortably completed his development and set about the weaknesses in the white camp.

8...g6 9 0-0 ♗g7 10 ♔h1 ♗f5 11 ♗c4?!

Kasparov also didn't like this one, giving 11 ♗e3 ♗xd3 12 ♕xd3 0-0 13 ♘xd7 ♘xd7 14 f5 as equal.

11...e6 12 ♗e2 h5 13 ♗e3 ♖d8 14 ♗g1 0-0

Solid enough, but 14...♘xe5!? 15 fxe5 ♘g4 is more enterprising, with ideas of ...♘xe5 and ...c6-c5. One possible continuation runs 16 ♕b1 c5 17 ♗b5+ ♔f8 18 d5!? ♖xd5! 19 ♘xd5 ♕xb5 20 ♘e3 ♘xe3 21 ♗xe3 ♗xe5, when Black has tremendous compensation for the exchange.

15 ♗f3 ♘d5

15...c5 would have been more forcing, putting immediate pressure on White's creaking centre. In his notes to the game Kasparov gives 16 ♕e2, but fails to mention 16...♕b4!, simultaneously hitting d4 and b2, which looks good for Black.

16 ♘xd5 exd5 17 ♗f2 ♕c7 18 ♖c1 f6 19 ♘d3 ♖fe8 20 b3 ♘b6 21 a4 ♘c8 22 c4 ♕f7 23 a5 ♗f8 24 cxd5 cxd5 25 ♗h4!? ♘d6

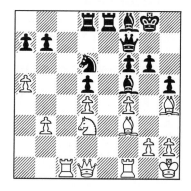

In a positional sense Kasparov had been totally outplayed. However, with both players approaching time-trouble Kasparov went into 'hustle mode', presenting Anand with many tactical problems, which the Indian GM failed to solve.

26 a6!? b6 27 ♘e5!?

This is the start of the confusion. Should Black accept the sacrifice?

27...♕e6

After 27...fxe5 28 fxe5 ♘e4 29 ♗xd8 ♖xd8 30 g4! hxg4 31 ♗xg4 ♗xg4 32 ♕xg4 ♘f2+ 33 ♖xf2 ♕xf2 34 ♕xg6+ ♗g7 35 ♕e6+ matters are far from clear, especially as 35...♕f7 allows 36 ♕xf7+ ♔xf7 37 ♖c7+.

28 g4! hxg4 29 ♘xg4 ♗g7

In time pressure Anand starts to make some second-rate moves. According to Kasparov 29...♗e7! would have kept the advantage after 30 ♘h6+ ♔g7 31 ♘xf5+ ♘xf5 32 ♖e1 ♕d6 33 ♗g3 ♖h8!

30 ♖c7 ♘e4?!

30...♗xg4 31 ♗xg4 f5! would have been better, as after 32 ♗xd8 fxg4 33 ♗h4 ♕e4+ 34 ♔g1 ♘f5 35 ♗f2 ♗xd4 Black has excellent value for the exchange.

31 ♘e3 ♗h3?! 32 ♖g1 g5?! 33 ♗g4 ♗xg4 34 ♕xg4 ♕xg4 35 ♖xg4 ♘d6 36 ♗f2 ♘b5 37 ♖b7 ♖e4 38 f5 ♖xg4 39 ♘xg4 ♖c8 40 ♖d7 ♖c2? 41 ♖xd5 1-0

The game has turned a full 180 degrees. After 41...♘c7 42 ♖d8+ ♔h7 43 ♖d7 ♘xa6 44 ♘xf6+ ♔h6 45 ♘e4 Black's position is hopeless. Another White victory, but from a theoretical standpoint, Black can have no complaints whatsoever.

Game 23
Zapata-Zarnicki
Matanzas 1993

---

1 e4 d5 2 exd5 ♕xd5 3 ♘c3 ♕a5 4 ♘f3 ♘f6 5 d4 c6 6 ♘e5 ♗e6 7 ♗c4 ♗xc4 8 ♘xc4 ♕d8 9 0-0

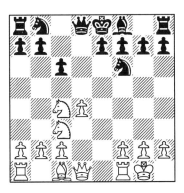

9...g6

Given that Black has problems defending e7 after this move, perhaps 9...e6 is a stronger option. Certainly after 9...e6 10 ♗f4 ♗e7 11 ♖e1 0-0 12 ♗e5 ♘bd7 13 ♕f3 b5 14 ♗xf6 gxf6 15 ♘e3 ♖c8 16 ♖ad1 ♔h8 17 ♘e4 ♖g8 18 a3 ♘b6 Black had no reason to complain in Daly-Prie, Linares Zonal 1995.

10 ♖e1 ♗g7 11 ♕e2! b5 12 ♘e5 0-0 13 ♗g5!? ♕xd4 14 ♖ad1 ♕b6 15 ♕f3 b4 16 ♘a4 ♕b5 17 b3

White has built up a very powerful initiative. Black now tries to diffuse some of the pressure by off-loading the extra pawn, but White retains a significant edge.

17...♘d5 18 ♘xc6 ♕xc6 19 ♕xd5 ♕xd5 20 ♖xd5 ♘c6 21 ♖c5 ♖ac8 22 ♖e4 h6 23 ♗e3

But not 23 ♗xe7? ♖fe8.

23...♖fd8 24 ♔f1 e5

see following diagram

---

25 ♖ec4 ♖d6 26 ♖xb4

Winning a pawn. The rest is downhill for Black.

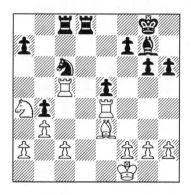

26...f5 27 Ἐbc4 f4 28 ἐc1 Ἐd1+ 29
ἐe2 Ἐxc1 30 Ἐxc6 Ἐxc6 31 Ἐxc6
e4 32 Ἐc4 g5 33 ἐc5 Ἐg1 34 g3
f3+ 35 ἐd2 Ἐg2 36 ἐe3 g4 37
ἐxe4 Ἐxh2 38 ἐf4 h5 39 ἐg5 ἐe5
40 ἐf5 ἐb2 41 c3 ἐc1 42 Ἐc7 1-0

Nothing can be done about ἐf6+,
followed by ἐg6 and Ἐf7 mate.

Game 24
Conquest-Hodgson
German Bundesliga 1995

**1 e4 d5 2 exd5 ἕxd5 3 ἐc3 ἕa5 4
d4 ἐf6 5 ἐc4 c6**

The actual move-order to this game
was 4 ἐc4 ἐf6 5 d4 c6.

Instead of 5...c6 Black can also try
the tricky 5...ἐg4. After 6 f3 ἐf5 7
ἐge2 c6 (7...h5!? may be an improvement: 8 ἐf4 e6 9 0-0 c6 10 ἐg3
ἐbd7 11 a3 ἐg6 12 ἐge4 ἕd8 gave
Black equality in T.Horvath-Borsos,
Zalakaros Open 1991) 8 g4 ἐg6 9 ἐf4
ἐbd7 10 h4 e5 11 h5! ἐf5 12 gxf5
exf4 13 ἕd3 ἕc7 14 ἕe2+ ἐe7 15
ἐd2 ἐb6 16 ἐb3 Ἐd8 17 0-0-0! Ἐxd4
18 ἕg2 White had a strong attack in
Yudasin-Oll, Dos Hermanas 1992.
6 ἐd2 ἕc7?!

I don't like the look of this with-
drawal. Black probably should be
content with 6...ἐf5. Then 7 ἐf3
leads to the main line 5 d4 ἐf5 6 ἐd2
c6 7 ἐc4, which is discussed in Chapters 1 and 2, while 7 ἐd5!? reveals one
of the points of delaying ἐf3. Following 7...ἕd8 8 ἐxf6+ Black is forced to
capture with a pawn. W.Watson-
Rogers, London 1987, continued
8...gxf6 9 ἐf4 ἕb6!? (9...e6 may be
stronger) 10 ἐb3 a5 11 a4 Ἐg8 12
ἐe2! ἐa6 13 0-0 ἐb4 14 ἐg3 e6 15
ἐf4 0-0-0 16 c3 ἐa6 17 ἐc2 ἐg6 18
ἐb3 ἐf5. Here Watson sacrificed the
b-pawn with 19 ἐc4!?, but Jonathan
Speelman recommends the simpler 19
Ἐa2!, intending ἐc4, with a plus for
White.

7 ἐf3 ἐg4 8 h3 ἐxf3 9 ἕxf3

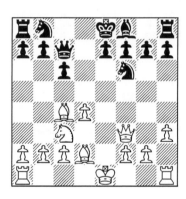

Once again we have reached a position which Black should really try to
avoid. White has the two bishops, is
ready to castle queenside and has the
simple plan of launching the kingside
pawns forward. In contrast, Black's
position lacks any real prospects of
counterplay.

**9...e6 10 0-0-0 ἐbd7 11 g4 ἐb6 12
ἐf1!**

An excellent square for the bishop. On b3 the bishop would only be prone to attack from ...a7-a5-a4.

12...♖d8 13 g5 ♘g8

An unnatural retreat, but 13...♘fd5 14 ♘e4! followed by c2-c4 would severely embarrass the knight.

14 h4!

Ignoring the attack on d4. Hodgson could not resist the offer.

14...♖xd4 15 ♘b5!!

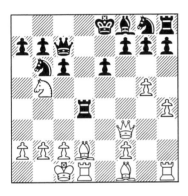

Commencing a Morphy style attack on the black king.

15...cxb5 16 ♗xb5+ ♘d7 17 ♗f4!

A star move, although Conquest admitted that the more sober 17 ♗c3 would have been equally effective.

17...♖xf4

17...♕xf4+ 18 ♕xf4 ♖xf4 19 ♖xd7 and Black will be checkmated, e.g. 19...a6 20 ♖hd1 axb5 (20...f6 21 ♖d8+ ♔f7 22 ♗e8+ ♔e7 23 ♖1d7 mate) 21 ♖d8+ ♔e7 22 ♖1d7 mate.

18 ♗xd7+ ♕xd7

18...♔e7 loses to 19 ♕a3+, but 18...♔d8 is more stubborn. Conquest gives 19 ♗xe6+ ♔e8 (19...♔e7 20 ♗c4!!) 20 ♗d7+ ♔d8 21 ♕e3 ♘e7 22 ♗b5+ ♔c8 23 ♖d7 as a winning line and there is no reason to argue with this.

19 ♕xf4 ♕c8

20 ♖h3!

Initiating the final decisive assault, and making good use of the earlier h2-h4!

20...♘e7

20...♗c5 21 ♖c3 followed by b2-b4 is good enough.

21 ♖f3 ♘f5 22 ♖c3

Now that the knight has been deflected, this move is a killer.

22...♗c5 23 ♖xc5 ♕xc5 24 ♕b8+ ♔e7 25 ♕xb7+ 1-0

25...♔e8 26 ♕d7+ ♔f8 27 ♕d8 is mate. A supreme attacking display by Conquest, but it has to be said that Black's opening play was rather slack.

Summary

Those wishing to revive the 5...♗g4 line need to find major improvement for Black on Game 17 (perhaps Soppe's 12...h6!?), as well as patching up the 9 h4 and 9 ♘c4 lines. 5...♘c6 is virtually refuted by 6 ♗d2, but 5...c6 could well overtake 5...♗f5 as the most popular choice in the future, especially as it takes some of the poison out of the early ♘e5 lines.

1 e4 d5 2 exd5 ♕xd5 3 ♘c3 ♕a5 4 d4 ♘f6

5 ♘f3 *(D)*
    5 ♗c4 - *game 24*
5...♗g4
    5...♘c6
        6 ♗d2 - *game 20*
        6 ♗b5 - *game 21*
    5...c6 6 ♘e5 ♗e6 *(D)*
        7 ♗d3 - *game 22*
        7 ♗c4 - *game 23*
6 h3 ♗h5 7 g4
    7 ♗d2 - *game 19*
7...♗g6 8 ♘e5 e6 9 ♗g2
    9 h4 - *game 18*
9...c6 10 h4 *(D)*
    10...♗e4 - *game 16*
    10...♘bd7 - *game 17*

5 ♘f3   6...♗e6   10 h4

CHAPTER FOUR

2...♛xd5: Fourth Move Alternatives

1 e4 d5 2 exd5 ♛xd5 3 ♘c3 ♛a5

Since both Black's theoretical standing and practical results have improved immensely in the lines arising after 1 e4 d5 2 exd5 ♛xd5 3 ♘c3 ♛a5 4 d4 ♘f6 5 ♘f3 (see Chapters 1 and 2), White players have recently been searching for fresh ideas in order to preserve an advantage out of the opening. In this chapter we shall examine some of these offbeat lines, as well as discussing various Black attempts to differ at move four.

One reasonable thought for White is the delay in moving the d-pawn. 4 d4 is a very natural move, but it is also quite committal and one can understand the benefits refraining from this advance. First, the black bishop on f5 may be blunted by a timely d2-d3, when White has no need to be concerned about the perennial weakness on c2. Second, if Black chooses to play ♗g4, there isn't the usual target pawn at d4. Finally, White gains a useful extra tempo to complete kingside development and castling. White generally does not have to fear Black claiming the centre with ...e7-e5, as Black is usually too undeveloped for this lunge to be effective.

Early games in this chapter see White playing the non-committal 4 ♘f3. Of course this can easily transpose to lines discussed earlier, but it retains its independence when White refrains from an early d2-d4. The plan starting with the unpretentious 5 ♗e2 is a deceptively annoying system that has caught a few people out. Black has many ways to play against it, but it is not clear which is the best procedure.

Of course, Black need not 'play ball' with 4 ♘f3 ♘f6; 4...♘c6 is an important alternative. This position often arises via the move order 1 e4 ♘c6 2 ♘f3 d5 3 exd5 ♛xd5 4 ♘c3 ♛a5. As we shall see, however, White has various ways of securing an advantage here.

Another important development has been 4 g3, introduced by the Lithuanian GM Eduard Rozentalis, who seems to manage to play g2-g3 against just about every single defence. Theoretically speaking, Black should be doing fine, but in practice results have been very favourable for White.

After 4 d4 Black's most important independent alternative is 4...e5. This, however, was dealt a crushing blow by a 'Vassily Ivanchuk novelty special' and the line has yet to recover. Other moves such as 4...♗f5 and 4...c6 are likely to transpose to main lines, whereas 4...g6 has some independent value.

Game 25
Short-Rogers
Tilburg 1992

---

1 e4 d5 2 exd5 ♕xd5 3 ♘c3 ♕a5 4 ♘f3 ♘f6 5 ♗e2!?

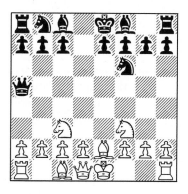

A peaceful looking move which does, however, contain a touch of venom.

5...♗g4

This move represents a fundamental method of development in the Scandinavian, so it can hardly be criticised. It does, however, fall in with White's plans and for that reason 5...g6 should also be considered carefully (see the next game). Another possibility is the development of the bishop on f5. Emms-Glek, Copenhagen Open 1995, continued 5...c6 6 0-0 ♗f5 7 b4! (a common theme in this line) 7...♕d8 8 b5 e6 9 ♖b1 ♗d6 10 bxc6 bxc6 11 ♗b2 h6 12 d3 ♗h7?! (too extravagant; 12...0-0 would have

been safer) 13 ♘e4! ♗e7 14 ♘xf6+ ♗xf6 15 ♘e5 ♕c7 16 ♘c4 ♗xb2 17 ♖xb2 and the 'Scandinavian bishop' was completely out of the game on h7. After 17...0-0 I should have played the powerful 18 ♕b1, which gives White a assured advantage, e.g. 18...♘d7 19 ♖b7 ♕d8 20 ♕b4 ♖b8 21 ♖b1 ♗g6 22 ♗f3 c5 23 ♕a3, when the queenside pawns are under extreme pressure.

6 h3 ♗h5 7 b4!

The sting in White's tail and the most aggressive way to play the position. 7 d4 ♘c6 8 0-0 0-0-0 would transpose to a favourable line for Black (see Game 36, note to Black's third move).

7...♕b6

Of course 7...♕xb4? 8 ♖b1 ♕d6 9 ♖xb7 is very advantageous to White, who threatens ♘b5.

8 0-0 c6

Perhaps this is an inaccuracy, as it gives White something to clasp onto on the queen's wing. According to Czech Grandmaster Pavel Blatny, Black should content himself with 8...e6, intending ...♗e7, when White has only a tiny plus.

9 ♖b1!

Very consistent. White plans b4-b5 in order to exchange pawns. This will leave White with an open b-file and Black with a weak c-pawn.

9...e6 10 b5 ♕c7 11 d4 ♗d6 12 bxc6 bxc6

Forced as 12...♘xc6 13 ♘b5 is very strong for White.

13 ♘e5 ♗xe2

13...♗xe5?! 14 ♗xh5 ♘xh5 15 dxe5 ♕xe5 16 ♗a3 gives White a strong initiative for the pawn, as 16...♕xc3 fails to 17 ♕d6!

14 ♕xe2 0-0 15 ♘c4 ♘bd7 16 ♘xd6 ♕xd6 17 ♖d1 ♘b6 18 ♖b3!

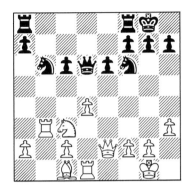

Threatening ♗a3, winning the exchange. White's advantage lies in the fact that his pieces are more active and he has a slightly superior pawn structure. Note that the rook on b3 may swing on the third rank to assist a kingside attack.

18...♖fe8 19 ♕f3 ♘bd5 20 ♘a4

Intelligently avoiding exchanges and eyeing the outpost on c5 (another consequence of the b4-b5 launch).

20...♕c7 21 c4 ♘e7

Black is slowly but surely getting pushed around. If now 21...♘b6? 22 ♗f4! something must drop, as 22...♕b7 loses to 23 c5.

22 ♘c5 ♘f5 23 ♗f4 ♕a5 24 ♗e5

see following diagram

24...♕xa2

Under intense strain, Rogers reasons that he may as well acquire a pawn for his troubles. All the same, White's attack now reaches deadly proportions.

25 ♗xf6 gxf6 26 ♘e4 ♔h8

26...♔g7 is well met by 27 g4.

27 ♘xf6 ♖g8

Equivalent to resignation, but 27...♖ed8 28 ♕h5 h6 29 ♕xf7 or 28...♔g7 29 ♖b7 ♖f8 30 ♘xh7 are terminal.

28 ♘xg8 ♖xg8 29 ♖b7 ♕xc4 30 ♖xf7 a5 31 ♕h5 ♘g7 32 ♕e5 ♕d5 33 ♖b1 h6 34 ♕f6 ♕g5 35 ♕xg5 hxg5 36 ♖bb7

White's two rooks rule the roost and are able to mop up the weak pawns at their leisure.

36...♔h7 37 ♖a7 ♔g6 38 g4! ♘e8 39 ♖fe7 ♔f6 40 ♖ed7 ♔g6 41 ♖xa5 ♘f6 42 ♖e7 ♘d5 43 ♖xe6+ ♔f7 44 ♖xc6 ♘f4 45 ♖a7+ 1-0

An excellent win by Short and a good advertisement for the ♗e2 system.

Game 26
Emms-Westerinen
Gausdal International 1995

---

1 e4 d5 2 exd5 ♕xd5 3 ♘c3 ♕a5 4 ♘f3 ♘f6 5 ♗e2 g6!?

This is a useful way to play against 5 ♗e2. Generally in the Scandinavian the kingside fianchetto is considered a little too extravagant for Black. Here, however, it is rather more justified. White's fifth move, while having many purposes, is not immediately threatening, so Black does have some extra time. In the same way 5...♘c6 should also be considered. White would normally like to play ♗b5 against this move, but here the bishop has already committed itself to e2. The game Seknadje-Relange, Brussels 1993, continued 6 0-0 ♗g4 7 h3 ♗h5 8 d3 e5!? 9 ♗d2 ♗e7 10 a3 ♕c5 11 b4 ♕d6 12 b5 ♘d8 13 ♘g5 ♗g6 14 ♘ge4 ♘xe4 15 dxe4 ♘e6 16 ♗e3 0-0 17 ♕xd6 ♗xd6 and Black had more than equalised due to White's queenside weaknesses, although White's play was hardly exemplary.

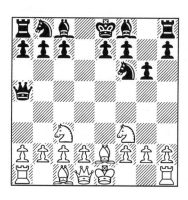

6 d4 ♗g7 7 0-0 0-0 8 ♘e5 ♗e6!

A common idea which we saw in Kasparov-Anand (Game 22). This theme is also popular in the Caro-Kann. Once the knight has committed itself to e5, the black bishop is able to rest peacefully on e6, not having to fear ♘g5. During the game I felt that Black had already equalised and since then nothing has made me change my mind.

9 ♗f3 c6 10 ♕e2 ♕a6 11 ♕e3

An ugly looking move, but exchanging queens would also present Black with no problems.

11...♖d8

11...♗f5 also looks good, hitting the unprotected c2-pawn.

12 ♖d1 ♘bd7 13 ♘d3 ♗g4?

This is slack. After a simple move such as 13...♖e8, Black is fine.

14 ♗xg4 ♘xg4 15 ♕xe7?

Here I missed a chance. The *intermezzo* 15 ♕e2! places Black in difficulty. After 15...♘gf6 16 ♕xe7 ♖e8 17 ♕b4 there is not enough compensation for the pawn.

15...♗xd4 16 ♗g5 ♕a5 17 ♘e2 ♗f6 18 ♗xf6 ♘gxf6 19 ♕e3 ♖e8 20 ♕f3 ♕d5 21 ♕xd5 ♘xd5

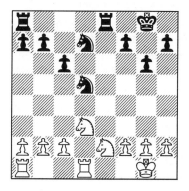

An absolutely level endgame has arisen. Stubbornly I played for the win and I did even manage to create some chances in my opponent's time-trouble, before throwing it all away again.

22 ♔f1 ♘e5 23 ♘xe5 ♖xe5 24 c4 ♘f6 25 ♘c3 ♖ae8 26 f3 ♖8e7 27 ♖d4 ♖d7 28 ♖ad1 ♖xd4 29 ♖xd4 h5 30 h4 ♔f8 31 ♔f2 ♔e7 32 g4 g5 33 hxg5 ♖xg5 34 ♔g3 hxg4 35 fxg4

♖g8 36 ♔f3 ♖h8 37 c5! ♘d7 38 ♘e4 ♘e5+?! 39 ♔f4 ♘g6+ 40 ♔g3

In time-trouble Black has carelessly manoeuvred the knight, leaving the queenside rather unprotected. Fearing ♘d6, Westerinen decided on a pawn lunge, but now White has significant winning chances.

40...b5 41 ♖d6 ♖c8 42 g5?

42 b3, to protect the c4-square, would have been much stronger, so that 42...♘e5 may be answered by 43 ♔f4! ♘g6+ 44 ♔f5, when White's active pieces ensure excellent winning chances.

42...♘e5! 43 b3 ♖d8

With the c-pawn protected, Black has time to contest the d-file.

44 ♖f6?! ♖d3+ 45 ♔f4 ♖d5 ½-½

If anything Black may now have a tiny edge, but my opponent was just relieved to take the draw after having to defend a tricky endgame.

Game 27
Fritsche-Hickl
German Bundesliga 1994

---

1 e4 d5 2 exd5 ♕xd5 3 ♘c3 ♕a5 4 ♘f3 ♘f6 5 ♗c4 c6

The most flexible move. Both main bishop moves have also been tried:

a) 5...♗f5 6 b4!? ♕b6 (6...♕xb4 7 ♘e5 e6 8 ♖b1 ♕c5 9 ♖b5 ♕d4 10 ♘e2 ♕d6 11 ♘xf7 ♔xf7 12 ♖xf5 is good for White) 7 0-0 e6 8 d3 ♗e7 (grabbing the b-pawn with 8...♗xb4 is still dangerous, e.g. 9 ♖b1 ♕a5 10 ♘b5 ♘a6 11 a3 ♗c5 12 ♗d2 ♕b6 13 ♘bd4!) 9 ♗f4 0-0 10 ♘b5 ♘a6 11 a3 ♘d5 12 ♗e5 ♗f6 13 ♕e1 and Black's poorly placed knight on a6 gave White a pull in Kharlov-Westerinen, Gausdal (Arnold Cup) 1992.

b) 5...♗g4 6 h3 ♗h5 7 ♕e2 ♘bd7 (7...e6 would have avoided the following storm) 8 g4 ♗g6 9 b4 ♕b6 10 h4 h6 11 h5 ♗h7 12 a4 c6 13 g5 hxg5 14 ♘xg5 ♗g8 15 a5 ♕c7 16 b5 cxb5 17 ♘xb5 ♕c6 18 ♖h3 and White's extremely energetic play was rewarded in Rohde-Seirawan, USA 1976.

6 0-0 ♗g4!

This pin is now rather awkward. Of course White can break it with h2-h3 and g2-g4, but this approach always has repercussions when the king is already consigned to the kingside.

7 h3 ♗h5 8 ♖e1 ♘bd7 9 d4 e6 10 ♗d2 ♕c7 11 ♗g5?!

Black has already achieved a comfortable position, and after this inaccuracy he can even go ahead and claim the initiative.

11...♗b4 12 g4 ♗g6 13 ♘e5 ♘xe5 14 dxe5?

Forcing the issue, but from a weak position. Black now wins a pawn.

14...♗xc3! 15 bxc3 ♘e4

---

see following diagram

---

16 ♗f4 ♘xc3 17 ♕f3 ♘d5 18 ♗g3

♕a5 19 ♗b3 ♖d8 20 ♗h4 ♖d7 21 ♖ad1 b5!

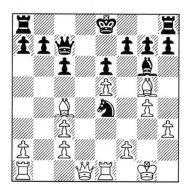

Securing the knight on d5. Black's position now plays itself.

22 ♗g5 0-0 23 h4 h6 24 ♗d2 ♕d8 25 h5 ♗h7 26 c4 bxc4 27 ♗xc4 ♘b6 28 ♗a5 ♖xd1 29 ♖xd1 ♕g5 30 ♗e2 ♗c2 31 ♖d2 ♗a4 32 ♕g3 ♘d5 33 ♖d4 ♕c1+ 34 ♔h2 ♗b5 35 ♗f3 ♕c5 36 ♖e4 ♗d3 37 g5 hxg5 38 ♖g4 ♕xa5 39 ♖xg5 ♕d2 40 ♖xg7+ ♔h8 41 ♗g2 ♗h7 42 ♕h4 ♕f4+ 0-1

A typical victory. Notice the 'Scandinavian bishop' playing an important part all the way through.

Game 28
Emms-L.Kristensen
Esbjerg 1996

---

1 e4 d5 2 exd5 ♕xd5 3 ♘c3 ♕a5 4 ♘f3 ♘c6 5 ♗b5

This move is even more convincing than the immediate 5 d4 ♗g4 6 ♗b5 0-0-0 7 ♗xc6 bxc6 8 ♕d3 f6 9 ♕c4 ♗d7 10 b4 ♕b6 11 ♖b1 e6 12 b5! of Van der Wiel-Schmidt, Aarhus 1983.

If now 5...♗g4 then White doesn't need to respond with 6 d4, but 6 h3! ♗h5 7 g4 ♗g6 8 ♘e5 with a clear

plus. The black bishop is therefore forced into a passive role.

5...♗d7 6 0-0

The most flexible move. 6 d4 transposes to the game after 6...a6!? 7 ♗xc6 ♗xc6 7 0-0, while the retreat 7 ♗e2!? was tried in the game Smagin-Vlassov, Moscow 1995. That clash continued 7...0-0-0 8 0-0 ♘f6 9 ♗d2 e5 10 dxe5 ♘xe5 11 ♘e4 ♕d5 12 ♘xf6 gxf6 13 ♗c3 ♕e6 14 ♘d4 ♕b6, with an unclear position which Black went on to win. After 6 d4 Black's best could well be the straightforward 6...0-0-0 7 0-0 ♘f6!, transposing to the line 3 ♘c3 ♕a5 4 d4 ♘f6 5 ♘f3 ♘c6 6 ♗b5 ♗d7 7 0-0 0-0-0 (see Game 21).

6...a6

A logical follow up to 5...♗d7. This line is a favourite of the Russian IM Vlassov. Black strives to claim the bishop pair, but does so at a serious development cost. Once again Black should possibly opt for 5...0-0-0 6 d4 ♘f6, transposing to the line considered in the previous note. In turn White could try 6 ♕e2!? or 6 ♖e1, reserving the development of the d-pawn to avoid handing Black a target in the centre.

7 ♗xc6 ♗xc6 8 d4 0-0-0 9 ♘e5 ♗e8

This is very unnatural, but it is the only way to retain the bishop pair. 9...♗d5? would have been a blunder due to 10 b4 ♕xb4 11 ♘xd5 ♖xd5 12 ♘xf7 winning material.

10 b4!

A powerful novelty. The b-pawn is a small price to pay in order to exploit the development superiority. Two other moves have also been played here:

a) 10 ♕f3 f6 11 d5!? e6!? 12 ♘c4 ♕c5 13 b3 b5 14 dxe6 ♗c6 15 ♕h3 ♘e7! 16 ♘a5 ♗a8 17 a3 ♕f5! 18 ♕e3 occurred in V.Ivanov-Vlassov, Moscow 1994. Black now went astray with 18...♘c6?, when White obtained the advantage with 19 ♘xc6 ♗xc6 20 e7 ♗xe7 21 ♕xe7. According to Ivanov Black should have played 18...♔b8!, when Black's raking bishop and White's weak c2-pawn counterbalance the pawn deficit.

b) 10 ♗e3 f6 11 ♘c4 ♕b4 12 ♕e2! b5 13 ♘d2 ♕xb2 14 ♘de4 e6 15 a4 ♕b4 16 axb5 axb5 17 d5 exd5 18 ♖a8+ ♔d7 19 ♕g4+ ♔e7 20 ♗c5+ ♕xc5 21 ♘xc5 ♖xa8 22 ♕e6+ and Black had to resign in Nikitin-Vlassov, St Petersburg 1995. Another poor advert for this system.

10...♕b6

Accepting the offer with 10...♕xb4 would have given White an awesome attack after 11 ♕f3 c6 12 ♖b1 ♕xd4 13 ♗f4. I don't fancy Black's chances of surviving that one!

11 ♗e3 e6

Paradoxically 11...♕xb4 is more playable here than on the previous move, as 11 ♕f3 is now impossible due to the undefended knight. Nevertheless White still keeps a strong initiative with 12 ♘e4 e6 13 ♖b1 ♕a4 14 ♕f3 (or 14 ♘c3 ♕a5 15 ♕f3!?).

12 ♖b1 f6?

This is just too provocative. 12...♘f6 had to be played, just to get some pieces out.

13 ♘c4 ♕c6 14 ♘a5! ♕xc3

Giving up the queen, but 14...♕d7 15 b5 produces a crushing attack.

15 ♖b3 ♗xb4 16 ♖xc3 ♗xc3

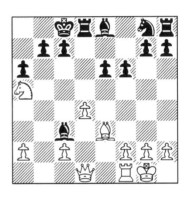

The material situation is roughly level, but Black is still woefully behind on the development front. It is easy to understand that the forthcoming sacrifice works in every variation.

17 ♘xb7! ♔xb7 18 ♕b1+ ♔a8 19 ♕b3 ♗xd4

19...♗a5 20 ♕a3 ♗b6 21 ♕f8! is a cute line. White rounds up the rook on h8.

20 ♗xd4 ♗b5

The recapture 20...♖xd4 fails to 21 ♕xe6 ♗b5 22 ♕c8+ ♔a7 23 ♕xc7+ ♔a8 24 ♕xg7, when the undeveloped rook is again 'slaughtered in its bed'.

21 c4 ♗c6 22 ♕a3 ♗b7 23 ♕c5 ♔b8 24 ♖b1 ♔c8 25 ♕a7 1-0

25...♗e4 26 ♖b8+ ♔d7 27 ♖xd8+ ♔xd8 28 ♕b8+ ♔d7 29 ♕f8 would have been a thematic finish.

Game 29
Rozentalis-Khalifman
Germany 1993

1 e4 d5 2 exd5 ♕xd5 3 ♘c3 ♕a5 4 g3

4...♘f6 5 ♗g2 c6

Ivanchuk's 5...e5 is considered in the next game.

6 ♘f3 ♗g4 7 0-0 e6 8 h3 ♗xf3

The game Kaminski-Jirovsky, Lazne Bohdanec 1996, portrays what may happen to Black if he refrains from capturing on f3. After 8...♗h5 9 d4 ♘bd7 10 g4! ♗g6 11 ♘h4 0-0-0 12 a3 ♘b6 13 ♘xg6 hxg6 14 ♕f3 ♖d7 (14...♖xd4 15 g5 ♘fd5 16 ♕xf7) 15 ♖b1 ♘bd5 16 b4 ♕c7 17 ♘a4 White's queenside assault inevitably turned out to be decisive.

9 ♕xf3 ♗e7

A year later at Wijk aan Zee, Sergei Tiviakov played exactly the same variation against Scandinavian expert Curt Hansen. At this point Hansen diverged with 9...♘bd7 10 a3 ♗e7 11

b3 0-0 12 ♗b2 ♖fd8 13 d4 ♖ac8 14 ♘d1 b5 15 ♘e3 ♕c7, when Black's position was extremely sound. In fact after 16 ♕e2 ♘b6 17 ♖fd1 a5 18 c4 they agreed a draw.

10 a3!? 0-0 11 ♖b1 ♕c7 12 b4 a6 13 d3 ♘bd7 14 ♗f4 ♗d6 15 ♗d2 a5 16 ♕e2

Here Rozentalis claims a small edge for White, although after 16...♖fe8 Black has no real weaknesses and can be reasonably satisfied with the outcome of the opening. Instead Khalifman permits the Lithuanian GM to drum up a substantial initiative.

16...♗e7? 17 f4 ♖fe8 18 g4 ♗f8 19 ♕f3 g6 20 ♔h1?

Rozentalis criticised this move afterwards, preferring the more direct 20 f5.

20...axb4 21 axb4 ♗g7 22 b5 ♖ac8?

Here Black misses his big chance. 22...♘d5 23 ♘e4 f5! blocks the white play on the kingside and gives Black excellent counter-chances.

23 bxc6 bxc6 24 ♘e2!

Concentrating all of his forces on the kingside. The position will gradually open up, when the bishop pair will flourish.

24...♛d6 25 ♘g3 ♛d5?!

Losing valuable time, although I must say that it is difficult to suggest an alternative.

26 ♛f2 ♛d6 27 f5 exf5 28 gxf5 c5 29 ♗f4! ♘e5

This is a nasty self-pin, but 29...♛d4 would have allowed 30 ♗b7 ♖cd8 31 ♗c7, picking up an exchange for nothing.

30 ♗g5 ♘ed7 31 ♖b7 ♛d4 32 ♘e4

White's pieces have now reached their prime attacking posts, and even the exchange of queens will not relieve Black of the increasing strain on his position.

32...♘xe4 33 ♗xe4 ♛xf2 34 ♖xf2 ♘e5 35 ♗d5 ♖b8 36 ♖a7 ♔h8

According to Rozentalis, Black should have tried 36...gxf5, although after the straightforward 37 ♖xf5 Black is still in a terrible way.

37 f6 ♗f8 38 ♗xf7

Capturing a very significant pawn, since the f-pawn proves to be a winner.

38...♘xf7 39 ♖xf7 h6 40 ♗d2 ♖e6 41 ♗c3 c4 42 dxc4 ♖e3 43 ♗d4 ♖xh3+ 44 ♔g2 ♖h5 45 ♖c7 ♖g5+ 46 ♔f1 ♖g4 47 c3 ♖b1+ 48 ♔e2 ♖g3 49 ♖f3!

Black still has a few tricks. 49 c5? ♖b2+ would have granted a perpetual check.

49...♖g2+ 50 ♔d3 ♖d1+ 51 ♔e4 ♖e1+ 52 ♖e3 ♖f1 53 c5 1-0

Black cannot deal with both the c-pawn and the f-pawn, e.g. 53...g5 54 c6 h5 55 ♖c8 ♔g8 56 c7. An impressive win from Rozentalis, demonstrating that 4 g3 is a dangerous weapon.

Game 30
Anand-Ivanchuk
London PCA Grand Prix (Blitz) 1995

1 e4 d5 2 exd5 ♛xd5 3 ♘c3 ♛a5 4 g3

4 b4!? inaugurates the Mieses Gambit. In the age of *Fritz* and *Chess Genius* these speculative gambits don't really hit the mark. Black should just grab the pawn and say 'thank you' with 4...♛xb4. After 5 ♖b1 ♛d6 6 ♘f3 ♘f6 7 d4 a6! Black has a sound enough position and one pawn more.

4...♘f6 5 ♗g2 e5!?

Even though this move was only tested out in a blitz game, one can assume, as it is Ivanchuk, that it had probably been thoroughly researched. On first inspection it does indeed look like a viable option.

6 ♘ge2 ♗d6 7 0-0 0-0 8 d4

Naturally White can keep the centre closed with 8 d3, but this should not pose too many problems for Black. After 8...c6 9 ♗g5 (perhaps 9 f4!?) 9...♘bd7 10 a3 h6 11 b4 ♛c7 12 ♗c1 a6 13 ♖b1 b5 14 a4 ♗b7 15 axb5?! (it was much better to keep the tension) 15...cxb5! 16 ♗xb7 ♛xb7 17 f3 ♘b6 18 ♘e4 ♗e7 19 ♘xf6+ ♗xf6 Black stood very well in Konopkova-M.Maric, Moscow Olympiad 1994.

8...♘c6 9 ♗g5 exd4 10 ♗xf6 dxc3 11 ♗xc3 ♛h5 12 ♘f4

Perhaps White should try 12 ♘d4 here. Then 12...♛xd1 13 ♖axd1 ♘xd4 14 ♗xd4 gives a favourable endgame, with Black's queenside under pressure. However, 12...♗g4 is much less accommodating as after 13 ♛d2 (13 f3

&d7) 13...&fd8! Black is okay, since 14 &xc6 &xg3! favours him.

12...&xd1 13 &axd1 &f5 14 &d2?!

14 &d3 is equal, but Ivanchuk had odds of the draw, so Anand was obviously trying to keep the game as unbalanced as possible. He succeeds in doing so, but only in Black's favour.

14...&xf4 15 gxf4 &ad8 16 &fd1?

Blundering a pawn, but 16 &xd8 &xd8 17 &c1 is also uninspiring.

16...&xc2 17 &xd8 &xd8 18 &xd8+ &xd8 19 &e5 c6 20 &h3 &e6 21 f5? &g5 22 &g4 &xf5!

Another pawn goes as 23 &xf5 allows 23...&f3+.

23 &e2 &e4 24 &b8 a6 25 f4 &e6 26 &f2 f5 27 &e3 h6 28 h4 g5 29 fxg5 hxg5 30 h5 &g7 31 a4 &h6 32 a5 &g7 33 &d4 c5+ 34 &xc5 &xh5 35 &b6 g4 ½-½

Of course Black is winning, but a draw was all that Ivanchuk required.

> ## Game 31
> ## Ivanchuk-Angelov
> *Varna 1987*

1 e4 d5 2 exd5 &xd5 3 &c3 &a5 4 d4 e5

Introduced by Adolph Anderssen, this is Black's most critical alternative to 4...&f6. Here is a brief summary of the other tries:

a) After 4...&c6? 5 d5 is just natural and strong. As 5...&b4 6 a3 &f5 7 &b5+ c6 8 axb4 &xa1 9 dxc6 wins for White, the knight is forced to an unfavourable square.

b) 4...g6 is hardly ever seen, but perhaps it is not that bad. 5 &f3 &g7 6 &c4 &f6 7 0-0 0-0 8 &e1 should give an edge for White, while also possible is the more aggressive 5 &f4 &g7 6 &d2, intending 0-0-0.

c) 4...&f5 and 4...c6 have no real independent value, as Black sooner or later plays ...&f6, transposing into main lines.

5 dxe5 &c6

5...&xe5+ was Anderssen's move in his match with Paul Morphy in 1858, but after 6 &e2 &b4 7 &f3 &xc3+ 8 bxc3 &xc3+ 9 &d2 &c5 10 &b1 &c6 11 0-0 Morphy had good compensation for the pawn and went on to win. 5...&c6 is an attempt to improve on Anderssen's line.

6 &f3 &b4 7 &d2 &g4 8 a3 &d4 9 &b5+!

A terrible blow for Black in this line. Other continuations have not established a clear edge for White:

a) 9 axb4?! ♕xa1! 10 ♗b5+ c6 11 ♕xa1 ♘xc2+ 12 ♔e2 ♘xa1 13 ♖xa1 cxb5 14 ♘xb5 is unclear.

b) 9 ♗e2 ♗xf3 10 ♗xf3 ♕xe5+ 11 ♔f1 ♗xc3 12 ♗xc3 0-0-0 is also not too bad for Black. Dolmadian-Angelov, Varna 1987, continued 13 ♗xd4 ♖xd4 14 ♕e2 ♕f6 15 g3 ♘h6 16 ♔g2? (16 c3! gives White an edge) 16...♖hd8!, when Black's control of the d-file gives an advantage.

9...c6

Ivanchuk's analysis runs 9...♘xb5? 10 axb4 ♕xb4 11 ♖a4 ♘xc3 (or 11...♗xf3 12 ♖xb4 ♗xd1 13 ♘xb5; 11...♕xb2 12 ♘xb5 ♗xf3 13 ♘xc7+) 12 ♖xb4 ♘xd1 13 ♖xg4 ♘xb2 14 ♖b4. In all lines White has a clear or winning superiority.

10 0-0!!

A dazzling concept. With everything hanging White throws another spanner into the works.

10...♗xf3!

10...cxb5 also favours White after 11 axb4 ♕xb4 12 ♘xb5!! ♕xb5 (12...♘xf3+ 13 ♕xf3!! wins for White) 13 ♘xd4 ♕d7 14 ♘f3 ♗xf3 15 gxf3 ♘e7 16 ♗b4 ♘d5 17 ♗d6 ♘f4 18 ♔h1!, when as well as being a pawn down, the black king is stranded.

11 axb4!

All the exclamation marks are Ivanchuk's! Here he gives another crazy variation which ends in a brilliant two-knight checkmate: 11 gxf3? ♗e7! 12 ♘d5 ♕xd2!! 13 ♘c7+ ♔f8 14 ♕xd2 ♘xf3+ 15 ♔g2 ♘xd2 16 ♘xa8 cxb5! 17 ♖fd1 ♗g5! 18 ♔g3 ♘e7! 19 f4

♘f5+ 20 ♔g4 ♘e3+ 21 ♔xg5 ♘f3+ 22 ♔h5 g6+ 23 ♔h6 ♘g4 mate!

11...♗xd1 12 bxa5 ♗xc2 13 ♗a4! ♘e7 14 ♗xc2 ♘xc2

The smoke has cleared somewhat and White is left with a very pleasant endgame. In particular, Black's knights have no support and are always in danger of being trapped.

15 ♖a4 ♖d8 16 ♘e4 ♘f5 17 g4 ♘fd4?!

Ivanchuk gives 17...♖d4!? as Black's last chance. He follows this up with 18 b3! ♘h4 (or 18...♖xa4 19 bxa4 ♘fd4 20 ♖b1 and the queenside pawns drop) 19 ♗c3 ♖d3 20 ♖c1 with a distinct plus, as Black's pieces are still clumsily placed.

18 ♘d6+! ♔e7

18...♖xd6 19 exd6 ♘f3+ 20 ♔g2 ♘xd2 21 ♖c1 snares the knight.

19 ♗c3 c5 20 ♘xb7 ♖d5 21 ♖c4 h5 22 ♖xc5 ♖xc5 23 ♘xc5 hxg4 24 ♔g2 ♘f3 25 ♖d1!

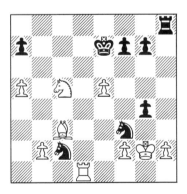

Giving up the h2-pawn, but White intends to round up the knight on c2.

25...♖xh2+ 26 ♔g3 ♔e8 27 ♘e4 ♖h6 28 ♔xg4 ♘h4 29 ♖c1 1-0

Finally the knight is trapped. A typically vibrant Ivanchuk game.

Summary

Of White's options here, lines with 4 ♘f3 ♘f6 5 ♗e2, together with Rozentalis's 4 g3, have proved to be the most dangerous weapons. Nevertheless, the well-prepared Black player should find enough defensive resources. On the other hand, Black's divergences from the main lines have not been too fruitful: both 4 ♘f3 ♘c6 and 4 d4 e5 are currently in need of restoration.

1 e4 d5 2 exd5 ♛xd5 3 ♘c3 ♛a5

4 ♘f3 *(D)*
    4 g3 ♘f6 5 ♗g2 *(D)*
        5...c6 - *game 29*
        5...e5 - *game 30*
    4 d4 e5 - *game 31*
4...♘f6
    4...♘c6 - *game 28*
5 ♗e2 *(D)*
    (5 ♗c4 - *game 27*)
5...♗g4 - *game 25*
5...g6 - *game 26*

4 ♘f3   5 ♗g2

5 ♗e2

CHAPTER FIVE

2...♛xd5: Second and Third Move Alternatives

1 e4 d5 2 exd5 ♛xd5

In this chapter we begin by examining other queen moves for Black. 3...♛d8 looks a little passive, but it does have some positive ideas, including a kingside fianchetto and the development of the king's knight to f5 via h6. Unfortunately there have been no important improvements for Black on the famous game between Bobby Fischer and Karl Robatsch (Game 32), which was annotated by Fischer in his *My Sixty Memorable Games*. More recently Black has played 3...♛d8 with the view of a more classical development (Game 33). This is a solid choice, but it allows White to develop freely and this usually leads to a comfortable edge.

3...♛d6 (Games 34 and 35) has been a regular choice of David Bronstein's, who has never been afraid to improvise in the opening. Black has some hidden resources in this line, as the game Toptshy-Donskysh proves. After 3...♛d6 4 d4 ♘f6 5 ♘f3 the critical response is 5...a6!, a seemingly extravagant move which has nevertheless proved difficult to overcome.

Other third move options for White are less logical than 3 ♘c3, but as always there are many transpositional possibilities. 3 d4 may be met in a number of ways, but perhaps the most critical move is 3...e5, as in the game De Firmian-Granda Zuniga (Game 36). White's other second and third move choices are discussed in Games 37.

1 e4 d5 2 exd5 ♛xd5 3 ♘c3 ♛d8 4 d4 g6

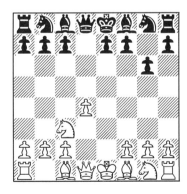

The most natural follow-up to 3...♛d8. The bishop will add extra pressure to the d4 pawn. 4...♘f6 is considered in the next game.

5 ♗f4!

Fischer's prescription. In comparison 5 ♘f3, while being very sensible, fails to present Black with as many problems. Then 6 ♗c4 ♘h6! sees the concept behind Black's opening: the knight will arrive at f5 to further increase the tension on the d-pawn. After 5 ♘f3 ♗g7 White should probably play Sokolsky's idea of 6 h3, to answer 6...♘h6 with 7 g4! However, Black can then return to classical development with 6...♘f6, when White has possibly lost 'half a tempo' with h2-h3. Nevertheless, White should still retain a small edge here.

5...♗g7 6 ♕d2! ♘f6

It turns out that the pawn is immune after all. 6...♕xd4 7 ♕xd4 ♗xd4 8 ♘b5 ♗b6 9 ♘xc7+ ♗xc7 10 ♗xc7 gives White the two bishops in a very pleasant endgame, while 6...♗xd4 7 0-0-0 ♘c6 8 ♗b5 ♗d7 9 ♘d5 e5 10 ♘f3 reaches a position where, in Fischer's words, 'Black will never get out of the opening alive'.

7 0-0-0 c6 8 ♗h6 0-0?

Fischer doesn't rate this move at all. He reckons that Black should play 8...♗xh6 9 ♕xh6 ♗f5 and aim to castle queenside.

9 h4 ♕a5 10 h5!

Simple and direct, this is right up Fischer's street.

10...gxh5

This looks extremely ugly, but already choices are not easy to recommend. Fischer presents two other ways for Black to succumb:

a) 10...♖d8 11 hxg6 fxg6 12 ♗xg7 ♔xg7 13 ♕h6+ ♔g8 14 ♘f3 and the threat of ♘g5 is formidable.

b) 10...♘xh5 11 ♗e2 ♘f6 12 ♗xg7 ♔xg7 13 ♕h6+ ♔g8 14 g4 ♖d8 15 g5 ♘h5 16 ♗xh5 gxh5 17 ♖xh5 ♗f5 and now 18 g6!, which would also be the winning move against 17...♕f5.

11 ♗d3

A significant move, preventing 11...♗f5 due to 12 ♕g5! These possible pins against the queen do not help Black at all.

11...♘bd7 12 ♘ge2 ♖d8

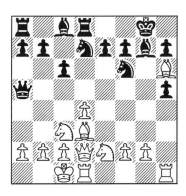

13 g4!

This is a real killer. White is able to expose the kingside without any further sacrifices.

13...♘f8

13...♘xg4 runs into 14 ♖dg1!, when White wins at least a piece, as there is no defence against the twin threats of ♖xg4 and f2-f3.

14 gxh5 ♘e6 15 ♖dg1 ♔h8

15...♔f8 also does not escape after 16 ♗xg7+ ♘xg7 17 ♕h6 ♘g4 18 ♕xh7, when White's attack crashes through.

16 ♗xg7+ ♘xg7 17 ♕h6 ♖g8 18 ♖g5 ♕d8 19 ♖hg1

see following diagram

19...♘f5

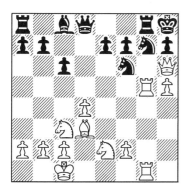

Timidly surrendering a piece. Fischer was obviously looking forward to the tougher defence 19...♛f8. His winning procedure would have been 20 d5! ♝d7 (20...cxd5 21 ♞xd5 ♞xd5 22 ♛xh7 mate) 21 d6! ♞f5 22 ♛xf8 ♖axf8 (22...♖gxf8 23 ♝xf5 h6 24 dxe7 ♖fb8 25 ♖g7 ♝xf5 26 ♖xf7 wins a piece) 23 ♝xf5 ♖xg5 24 ♖xg5 h6 25 dxe7 ♖b8 26 ♖g3 ♝xf5 27 ♖f3 and finally Black can resign.

20 ♝xf5 1-0

A powerful game and the main reason for the virtual disappearance of 4...g6 from tournament play.

> *Game 33*
> **Chandler-Santo Roman**
> *Cannes (One-Hour Team Ch.) 1992*

---

1 e4 d5 2 exd5 ♛xd5 3 ♞c3 ♛d8 4 d4 ♞f6

This is safer, but less critical than 4...g6. White should be able to maintain the advantage in a number of ways.

5 ♞f3 ♝g4

The only other natural move would have been 5...♝f5. White could then proceed in a straightforward

manner with 6 ♝c4, or try 6 ♞e5 e6 7 g4 ♝e4 (7...♝g6 8 ♝g2 c6 9 h4 leaves Black in big trouble, as 9...h6 10 ♞xg6 fxg6 is hardly desirable) 8 ♞xe4 ♞xe4 9 ♝g2 ♞d6. In the game Ochoa de Echaguen-Hernando, Spanish Team Championship 1995, White continued with the enticing 10 ♝xb7!? (10 ♛e2, preparing an eventual 0-0-0, is enough for a small edge) 10...♞xb7 11 ♛f3 ♛d5 12 ♛xf7+ ♚d8 13 ♝g5+ ♚c8 14 ♛e8+ ♞d8 15 ♛xd8+ ♛xd8 16 ♝xd8 ♝b4+ 17 c3 ♖xd8 18 cxb4 ♖xd4 19 f3 ♖xb4 20 0-0-0 with a slightly better endgame, which was eventually converted into the full point.

6 h3 ♝h5

6...♝xf3 timidly relinquishes the two bishops, without any real compensation: 7 ♛xf3 c6 8 ♝e3 e6 9 ♝d3 ♞bd7 10 0-0 ♛c7 11 ♞e2 ♞d5 12 ♝d2 ♞b4 13 ♝c4 ♞f6 14 a3 ♞bd5 15 ♝b3 b5 16 ♖ac1 was enough for a pull in And.Tzermiadianos-Makropoulou, Greek Championship 1994. In my view 9 0-0-0 is even stronger, reserving the placement of the light-squared bishop, and preparing g2-g4.

7 g4 ♝g6 8 ♞e5 e6 9 ♝g2 c6 10 0-0!?

Deciding to maintain the knight on e5. 10 ♞xg6 hxg6 11 ♛d3 would have given White a small, but definite plus.

10...♞bd7 11 ♛e2 ♞xe5 12 dxe5 ♞d7 13 ♞e4

---

see following diagram

13...h5

Black does well to resist the temptation to grab the e-pawn. 13...♞xe5 14 ♝g5 offers White obvious compensation. One line given by Blatny runs

14...f6 15 ♖ad1 ♘d7 (15...♕c7 16 ♘xf6+ gxf6 17 ♗xf6 ♗g7 18 ♗xg7 ♕xg7 19 f4, intending f4-f5) 16 ♗xf6 gxf6 17 ♖xd7 ♔xd7 18 ♖d1+ ♔e7 19 ♖xd8 ♖xd8 20 ♘c5 with a winning advantage.

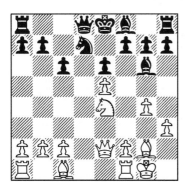

14 ♗f4 hxg4 15 hxg4 ♕a5 16 ♖ad1 0-0-0

Once again, grabbing the pawn is too risky: 16...♘xe5 17 ♘d6+ ♗xd6 18 ♖xd6 ♘d7 19 ♖fd1 ♘f6 20 ♖xc6! bxc6 21 ♗xc6+ ♔f8 (21...♔e7 22 ♗d6+ wins) 22 ♗xa8 ♖h4 23 ♗f3, when the extra pawn, coupled with Black's dodgy king, gives White a won position.

17 a3 ♗e7

No third time lucky! According to Blatny, 17...♘xe5 18 b4! ♕c7 19 ♖xd8+ ♔xd8 20 ♖d1+ ♔c8 21 ♘c5 ♗d6 22 ♖xd6 ♕xd6 23 ♗xe5 wins, and I agree with him.

18 ♘d6+ ♗xd6 19 ♖xd6

Things seem to be running quite smoothly for White, but in fact this is a typically resolute Scandinavian position. Black has managed to exchange two pairs of minor pieces, leaving the 'Scandinavian bishop', which, together with the queen, exerts pressure

on the White's queenside.

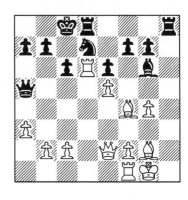

19...♘b6 20 c4 ♕a4

A useful move. The queen plans to filter into the light squares.

21 ♖c1 ♕b3 22 ♗g5 ♗d3 23 ♕f3 ♖xd6 24 exd6 f6

White has obtained a dangerous passed pawn on d6, but the position still remains totally unclear due to Black's active pieces. Chandler now felt obliged to enter more complications in order to maintain the initiative.

25 ♗xf6

25 ♗e3?! ♗xc4 26 ♖c3 ♕xb2 27 ♗xb6?? fails to 27...♕b1+.

25...gxf6 26 ♖c3 ♕xb2 27 ♖xd3 ♘d7 28 ♖d1 ♖g8 29 ♖e1 ♘c5 30 ♕e3 ♕b6 31 ♗f3 e5 32 ♔f1 ♘e6 33 ♕h6 ♕b3 34 ♕h7

In my opinion 34 ♕xf6! ♕xc4+ 35 ♔g1 ♘g5 36 ♗d1! is a good winning try here, as Black cannot utilise his apparent initiative, and White has been able to snatch a valuable pawn, while also leaving the e-pawn weak.

34...♖g7 35 ♕f5 ♕xc4+ 36 ♗e2 ♕d5 37 ♗f3 ♕c4+ 38 ♔g1

Considering that it was a rapidplay game, I imagine that Chandler could well have been trying to hustle his opponent here. Otherwise he may have opted for 38 ♗e2 ♛d5 39 ♗f3, which leads to a repetition.

38...♔d7 39 ♖b1

39 ♛xf6 ♖xg4+! 40 ♗xg4 ♛xg4+ leads to a draw by perpetual check, as 41 ♔f1 ♛h3+ 42 ♔e2 ♘f4+ is no way out.

39...b5 40 a4 a6 41 axb5 axb5 42 ♖d1

Now 42 ♛xf6 allows Black to force the exchange of queens with 42...♛f4! 43 ♛xf4 ♘xf4, and the d-pawn will drop.

42...♛c3 43 ♗e2

43...b4??

A terrible blunder, which invites White's bishop 'around the back'. After 43...e4!, intending ...♛e5, Black would have been firmly in control.

44 ♗a6! b3 1-0

45 ♗c8+! ♔xc8 46 d7+ and 47 ♛xe6 is terminal. 44...♛b3 would have been a sterner defence, but White still wins after 45 ♖c1! ♛d5 46 ♗c4 ♛xd6 47 ♖a1, as Black has no reasonable way to defend against the threat of ♖a7+. A strange end to a very eventful game.

Game 34
Toptshy-Donskych
Correspondence (ICCF Cup) 1992

1 e4 d5 2 exd5 ♛xd5 3 ♘c3 ♛d6!? 4 d4 ♘f6 5 ♘f3 a6

This forms part of David Bronstein's idea. Black takes time out to exclude ♘b5 and ♗b5. The alternative 5...♗g4 will be examined in the next game.

6 ♗e3

Preparing to castle long, which is the most ambitious plan in this position. Bronstein has had some experience in the quieter variation 6 ♗e2 e6 7 0-0:

a) 7...♘bd7 8 ♗g5 c5 9 ♗h4 cxd4 10 ♘xd4 ♗e7 11 ♗g3 ♛b6 12 ♘b3 0-0 13 a4 gave White a substantial advantage in Hartman-Bronstein, Wrexham 1995. The white bishop on g3 controls the important h2-b8 diagonal, leaving the black queen without a good post.

b) 7...♗e7 was Bronstein's new deviation in Rozentalis-Bronstein, Reykjavik Open 1996. After 8 ♘e5 ♘c6 9 ♘xc6 ♛xc6 10 ♗f3 ♛d6 11 g3 0-0 12 ♗f4 ♛d8 13 ♛d2 White still looks to be better, but Bronstein managed to relieve the pressure with 13...♘d5 14 ♖fe1 ♘xf4 15 ♛xf4 ♖b8 16 ♖ad1 b5 17 ♘e4 ♗d6 18 ♛e3 b4 19 ♘c5 a5 20 ♗g2 ♗d7 21 f4 ♗b5 22 a4 bxa3 23 bxa3 a4 24 ♛c3 ♛e7 25 ♖b1 ♖b6 26 ♖b4 ♖fb8 27 ♛e3 ♛e8 28 c3, when a draw was agreed.

6...♘c6 7 ♛d2 ♗f5

An improvement over the old game Karpov-Lutikov, USSR 1979,

which continued 7...♗g4 8 ♘g5 e5 9 d5 ♘b4 10 f3 ♗f5 11 ♘ge4 ♕d7 12 0-0-0 c6 13 dxc6 with a big advantage to White.

8 a3 e6 9 ♗c4 ♗e7 10 ♘h4 ♗g4 11 h3 ♗h5 12 g4 ♗g6 13 ♘xg6 hxg6 14 0-0-0 ♘d5 15 ♘xd5 exd5 16 ♗f1 0-0-0 17 ♗g2 ♘a7! 18 f4 ♕b6 19 ♕d3 ♘c6

Black has overcome his opening difficulties and now intends to create counterplay with ...♘c6-a5-c4, inducing White into taking some central action.

20 c4 dxc4 21 ♕xc4 ♖d7! 22 ♖d3 ♕b5?!

The queen turns out to be misplaced here. 22...♗f6 23 ♖hd1 ♖hd8 is more natural, ganging up on the d-pawn.

23 ♕c2 ♗d6 24 ♔b1 ♖e8 25 ♗f3 ♖de7 26 ♗d2 ♘d8 27 f5

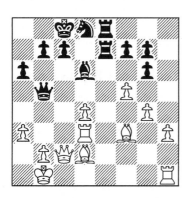

White's isolated d-pawn is now under no threat whatsoever, while the position is gradually opening up in favour of the two bishops.

27...gxf5 28 ♖b3 ♕d7 29 ♕d3! ♕a4

Retaining the pawn with 29...f4 succumbs to 30 ♗xb7+ ♘xb7 31 ♕xa6, when Black has no defence.

30 ♕xf5+ ♖d7! 31 ♔a2 g6

After 31...♕xd4 32 ♗c3 ♕f4 33 ♕xf4 ♗xf4 34 ♗xg7 the two bishops, together with the menacing passed h-pawn, give White a sizeable advantage.

32 ♕d3 ♗c5 33 d5 ♖d6?! 34 ♖c1 ♕d4 35 ♕c2 ♗b6 36 h4!

Black has made a series of inaccurate moves that have allowed White to secure total control of the position. White now embarks on a simple plan of creating a passed h-pawn, in order to further stretch Black's resources.

36...♔b8 37 h5 gxh5 38 gxh5 ♖xd5

Black panics and gives up an exchange. However, it is difficult to recommend a worthy alternative.

39 ♗xd5 ♕xd5 40 ♕d3! ♗d4

Black cannot grab the h-pawn: 40...♕xh5 41 ♖xb6 cxb6 42 ♕d7 ♕h8 43 ♗f4+ ♔a7 44 ♖c8 and the threats against the black king are decisive.

41 ♕c4 ♕d6?

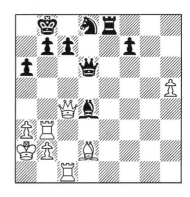

Another error, which puts Black out of his misery.

42 ♗b4 ♕c6 43 ♕xc6 ♘xc6 44 ♖xc6! bxc6 45 ♗c5+ 1-0

After a brief tactical flurry White emerges a whole piece to the good.

Game 35
Bologan-Muse
Berlin Open 1995

1 e4 d5 2 exd5 ♕xd5 3 ♘c3 ♕d6 4 ♘f3 ♘f6 5 d4 ♗g4

In conjunction with 3...♕d6, this move is not particularly effective.

6 h3 ♗xf3

When the bishop retreats to g6, the queen is unfavourably placed on d6, compared to a5. First, there is no useful pin on the c3 knight, and second the queen can be harassed by ♗f4: 6...♗h5 7 g4 ♗g6 8 ♘e5 c6 9 ♗f4! ♘d5 10 ♕d2 ♘xf4 11 ♕xf4 ♘d7 12 0-0-0 ♘xe5 13 dxe5 ♕c7 14 ♗d3 ♗xd3 15 ♖xd3 g6 16 ♘e4 gave White a menacing initiative in Psakhis-Sygulski, Yurmala 1987.

7 ♕xf3 c6 8 ♗e3 e6 9 0-0-0 ♕c7 10 ♔b1 ♘bd7 11 ♗c1!

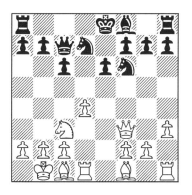

Model strategy by Bologan. White keeps the bishops on their original squares, where they can influence the game without becoming targets for the black knights. Meanwhile White is able to gain further ground by surging forward with the g- and h-pawns.

In general Black should aim to avoid these types of situation, as there is no apparent compensation for the lack of space and bishop pair.

11...♘b6 12 g4 h6 13 h4 0-0-0 14 ♗h3 ♗d6 15 ♘e2 ♘fd5 16 b3!

Preparing c2-c4, after which the black knights will have no safe ground.

16...c5 17 c4 ♘b4 18 ♗b2 ♖hg8 19 ♘c3 a6 20 ♘e4 cxd4?

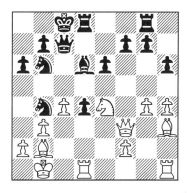

Dropping a piece, although Black's position was already very difficult.

21 c5! ♗e5

21...♗xc5 22 ♘xc5 ♕xc5 23 ♖c1 pins and wins the queen.

22 a3!

Less accurate is 22 cxb6 ♕c2+ 23 ♔a1 d3, when White is forced to play 24 ♖b1.

22...♘4d5 23 cxb6 ♕xb6 24 ♔a2 ♔b8 25 ♖c1

Black's two pawns provide insufficient compensation for the piece. Although White's winning process is quite lengthy, the conclusion is never in any doubt.

25...♖c8 26 ♖hd1 f6 27 ♗f1 ♖gd8 28 ♗c4 ♘f4 29 ♗d3 ♖xc1 30 ♖xc1 ♖c8 31 ♖xc8+ ♔xc8 32 ♘d2 ♕c5

33 ♘c4 ♗c7 34 ♗e4 b5 35 ♘d2 a5 36 ♗d3 f5 37 gxf5 exf5 38 ♗b1 g6 39 ♘f1 ♘d5 40 h5! ♘c3+ 41 ♗xc3 dxc3 42 ♘e3 ♗d6

This looks dangerous but...

43 b4! axb4 44 ♕a8+ ♔c7 45 hxg6 b3+

45...bxa3 46 g7 wins, as Black has no way to continue his 'attack' .

46 ♔xb3 c2 47 ♗xc2 ♗e5 48 ♕a5+ 1-0

Black is now just a clear piece down.

Game 36
De Firmian-Granda Zuniga
Amsterdam 1996

---

1 e4 d5 2 exd5 ♕xd5 3 d4

White aims to omit or at least delay ♘c3. 3 d4, however, presents Black with active possibilities.

3...e5!?

Directly challenging White's centre. Other ways include

a) 3...♘f6 will transpose to normal lines after 4 ♘c3 ♕a5 or 4 ♘f3 ♗g4 (see Chapter 8).

b) 3...♘c6 transposes to a line of the Nimzowitsch Defence, which arises after 1 e4 ♘c6 2 d4 d5 3 exd5!? ♕xd5. This line is not considered dangerous for Black: *ECO* gives 4 ♘f3 ♗g4 5 ♗e2 0-0-0 6 ♘c3 ♕a5 7 ♗e3 ♘f6 8 ♘d2 ♗xe2 9 ♕xe2 ♕f5 10 ♘b3 e5 11 0-0-0 exd4 12 ♘xd4 ♘xd4 13 ♗xd4 ♗c5 resulting in an equal position.

4 dxe5

4 ♘f3, maintaining the tension, deserves careful consideration: 4...exd4 5 ♘xd4 ♘f6 (5...♗c5!?) 6 ♘c3 ♗b4 7

♕e2+ ♕e4 8 ♗d2 ♕xe2+ 9 ♗xe2 c6 10 0-0-0 0-0 11 a3 ♗a5 12 h3 ♘bd7 13 g4 ♖d8 14 ♘b3 ♗c7 15 f4 ♘b6 16 f5 gave White a pleasant ending in Sevillano-Wahls, Biel Open 1993.

4...♕xd1+

This is much more dynamic than 4...♕xe5+, when the black queen is prone to attack in the centre of the board. Ziatdinov-G.Welling, Amsterdam (Donner Memorial) Open 1994, continued 5 ♗e2 ♗g4 6 ♗e3 ♗xe2 7 ♕xe2 ♘e7 8 ♘c3 ♘bc6 9 ♘f3 ♕e6 10 0-0-0 (White is already clearly better) 10...a6 11 ♖he1 ♖d8 12 ♖xd8+ ♔xd8 13 ♘g5 ♕g6 14 ♕c4 ♔e8 15 ♗f4 h6 16 ♘ge4 ♔d8 17 ♘c5 ♔c8 18 ♘xa6! bxa6 19 ♕xa6+ ♔b8 20 ♗xc7+ ♔xc7 21 ♘b5+ ♔d7 22 ♕b7+ ♔e8 23 ♕c8+ and Black had to resign as 24 ♘c7 will be mate.

5 ♔xd1 ♘c6 6 f4!?

Ambitiously seeking to maintain the pawn, but in return granting Black plenty of counterplay. Reasonable alternatives include:

a) 6 ♗b5 ♗d7 7 ♗xc6 (7 ♗f4 0-0-0 8 ♘d2 ♘xe5 9 ♗xd7+ ♘xd7 is equal) 7...♗xc6 8 ♘f3 ♗xf3+ 9 gxf3 0-0-0+ 10 ♔e2 ♖e8 11 f4 f6 and Black regains the pawn.

b) 6 ♘f3 ♗g4 7 ♗f4 ♘ge7 8 ♗b5 0-0-0+ 9 ♘bd2 ♗xf3+ 10 gxf3 ♘xe5! 11 ♗xe5 ♖d5 12 ♗c4 ♖xe5 13 ♗xf7 ♘c6 14 f4 ♖e7 15 ♗d5 ♘b4 16 ♗c4 g6 17 c3 ♘c6 18 ♖e1 ♖xe1+ 19 ♔xe1 ♗h6 20 ♘e4 ♗xf4 21 h3 and the players agreed a draw in Orel-Marinsek, Bled Open 1993.

6...♗f5 7 c3 0-0-0+ 8 ♔e1 f6 9 ♗b5 fxe5 10 ♗xc6 bxc6 11 fxe5 ♗c5 12 ♘f3

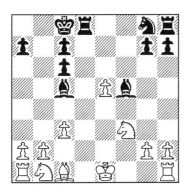

12...♘f6!

Possibly De Firmian missed this shot.

13 ♗g5?!

13 exf6 ♖he8+ 14 ♔f1 ♗d3 is mate. In my opinion White should throw extra wood on the fire with 13 b4! ♗b6 14 c4! (planning c4-c5) 14...♗c2! and now:

a) 15 ♘bd2 ♗e3! 16 exf6 ♖he8 17 f7 (17 ♘e4 ♗xc1 18 ♖xc1 ♗xe4 19 f7 ♖e7 is better for Black) 17...♗d4+! 18 fxe8♛ ♖xe8+ 19 ♘e4 ♗xa1 and Black is slightly better.

b) 15 ♗d2! ♘g4! (Black has to play actively) 16 c5 ♘xe5! 17 ♘xe5 (17 cxb6 ♘xf3+ 18 gxf3 cxb6! and White cannot prevent the deadly ...♖he8+) 17...♖he8 18 cxb6 ♖xe5+ 19 ♔f2 ♗xb1 20 ♗f4 (20 ♗c3 ♖f8+ 21 ♔g1 ♖e3 22 bxa7 ♔b7 23 ♖xb1 ♖xc3 and Black's active rooks still give him an edge) 20...♖f5 21 bxa7 ♔b7 22 ♖hxb1 (22 ♔g3 ♖d3+ 23 ♔g4 ♖d4 24 g3 ♗d3!) 22...♖xf4+ 23 ♔g1 ♔xa7 reaching an endgame that should be drawn.

13...h6 14 ♗h4 g5 15 ♗f2 ♗xf2+ 16 ♔xf2 ♘g4+ 17 ♔g3 h5! 18 h4?

White's last chance to save the game was the apparently greedy 18

♘xg5. After 18...h4+ 19 ♔f4 ♖df8 20 ♘d2! (the only move, but a good one!) 20...♗e6+ 21 ♔e4 ♗f5+ 22 ♔f4 both sides should be content with the perpetual check (22 ♔f3 ♖hg8 23 ♘ge4 ♘xe5+ 24 ♔e3 ♖xg2 favours Black).

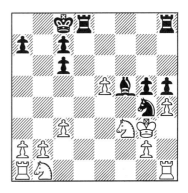

18...gxh4+ 19 ♘xh4 ♗h7 20 ♘f3 ♖hg8 21 ♖xh5

Desperation, but after 21 ♔h4 ♘f2 22 ♖f1 ♖g4+ 23 ♔xh5 ♗f5, Black mates with ...♖h8.

21...♘f6+ 22 ♖g5 ♘e4+ 23 ♔h4 ♘xg5 24 ♘xg5 ♖d1 25 e6 ♖g1 26 ♘d2 ♖xa1 27 ♘df3 ♗e4 28 ♘d4 c5 29 ♘b3 ♖g1 0-1

Game 37
Thorsteinsson-Tisdall
Reykjavik Open 1988

---

1 e4 d5 2 ♘c3

The most significant second move alternative. Other lines include:

a) 2 e5?! grants Black a very comfortable game after 2...♗f5 or 2...c5. One practical example continued 2...c5 3 c3 ♘c6 4 d4 cxd4 5 cxd4 ♗f5 6 ♘c3 e6 (Black has an excellent version of the French Advance, where the bishop is outside the pawn chain) 7 a3?! ♕b6 8 ♘f3 ♗g4 9 ♗e2? ♗xf3 10 ♗xf3 ♕xd4 11 ♕b3 ♕xe5+ 12 ♘e2 ♕c7 13 0-0 ♘f6 14 ♗g5 ♗e7 and Black was just two pawns up in McLafferty-Watkins, Scotland 1994.

b) 2 d4 is a multi-transpositional move. After 2...dxe4 we have the Blackmar-Diemer Gambit. Also Black has the choice of the Caro-Kann (2...c6), the French (2...e6) and the Nimzowitsch (2...♘c6). Scandinavian players may prefer 2...dxe4, which does win a pawn after all!

2...dxe4

The advance 2...d4 is also not bad. After 3 ♘ce2 e5 4 ♘g3, 4...♗e6! is an important move, preventing ♗c4. Casper-Maus, German Bundesliga 1992, continued 5 ♗e2 ♘c6 6 ♗b5!? ♘ge7 7 d3 ♕d6 8 ♗d2 g6 9 h3 ♗g7, and Black had equalised.

3 ♘xe4 ♘d7

As you would expect, Black has other reasonable tries here:

a) 3...♕d5!? offers White the chance to return to main lines with 4 ♘c3, which should probably be taken. Kenworthy-Prie, London-Paris 1994, continued instead 4 ♕f3?! ♘c6 5 ♘e2 (5 ♘f6+ ♘xf6!) 5...f5 6 ♕h5+ (6 ♘g5 ♕xf3 7 ♘xf3 e5) 6...g6 7 ♕4c3 ♕c5 8 ♕h4 e5 9 d3 f4 10 f3 ♗e7 11 ♕f2 ♕xf2+ 12 ♔xf2 ♘b4!, and Black won.

b) 3...♗f5 4 ♕f3!? (4 ♘g3 ♗g6 5 d4 reaches a ...♗f5 Caro-Kann [1 e4 c6 2 d4 d5 3 ♘c3 dxe4 4 ♘xe4 ♗f5 5 ♘g3 ♗g6], where Black has managed to omit ...c7-c6, which effectively grants an extra tempo) 4...♗g6 (4...♕d5 5 ♘d6+ ♕xd6 6 ♕xf5 claims the bishop pair and possibly a small plus) 5 c3 e5

6 ♗c4 ♗e7, intending ...♘c6 followed by ...♘f6, should be okay for Black.

4 d4 ♘gf6 5 ♘g5!? e6 6 ♗d3 ♗d6

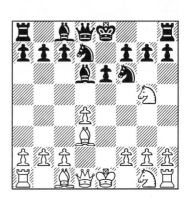

We have reached a position that is very similar to a variation of the 4...♘d7 Caro-Kann. The difference here is that Black has an extra tempo, because he has not played ...c7-c6.

7 ♘1f3 h6 8 ♘xe6?

Often in the Caro-Kann this can prove to be an enticing sacrifice. Here, however, Black's extra tempo allows him to consolidate the piece advantage effortlessly. Much healthier was 8 ♘e4 ♘xe4 9 ♗xe4 ♘f6 10 ♗d3 c5 with an equal position.

8...fxe6 9 ♗g6+ ♔e7 10 0-0 ♘f8 11 ♗d3 b6 12 c4 ♗b7 13 ♗d2 c5 14 ♗c3 cxd4 15 ♘xd4 ♔f7 16 ♖e1 ♗c5 17 ♘c2 ♕c7 18 b4 ♕f4! 19 ♘e3

19 bxc5 ♘g4 simultaneously attacks f2 and h2.

19...♗d6 20 ♗xf6 ♕xh2+ 21 ♔f1 gxf6 22 c5 ♖g8! 23 cxd6 ♖xg2 24 ♘g4

24 ♘xg2 ♕xg2+ 25 ♔e2 ♗f3+ picks up the queen.

24...♖g1+ 0-1

If 25 ♔e2 then 25...♖xg4 wins.

Summary

It seems that these earlier alternatives are less important than those studied in previous chapters. 3...♛d8 and 3...♛d6 are certainly playable, but don't really challenge White in the way that 3...♛a5 does. Likewise, after 3 d4 and 3 ♘f3 Black can generally choose between transposing to main lines or entering independent paths, which have proved to be fully satisfactory.

1 e4 d5

2 exd5
>   2 ♘c3 - *game 37*

2...♛xd5 3 ♘c3 *(D)*
>   3 d4 - *game 36*

3...♛d8
>   3...♛d6 4 d4 ♘f6 5 ♘f3 *(D)*
>>   5...a6 - *game 34*
>>   5...♝g4 - *game 35*

4 d4 *(D)*
>   4...g6 - *game 32*
>   4...♘f6 - *game 33*

3 ♘c3	*5 ♘f3*	*4 d4*

CHAPTER SIX

2...♘f6: Main Line with c2-c4

1 e4 d5 2 exd5 ♘f6 3 d4 ♘xd5 4 c4

The variation 3 d4 ♘xd5 4 c4 is the most common choice for White after 2...♘f6, and it is easy to see why it is so popular. White makes no attempt to hang on to the pawn as with 3 c4 and 3 ♗b5+, preferring just simple development. A tempo is gained by attacking the knight with c2-c4 and the d4/c4 pawn front ensures a comfortable space advantage.

The black knight normally retreats to b6, so that after ...g7-g6 and ...♗g7, the bishop can strike unimpeded at the white centre, and this set-up is the subject of Games 38-43. White has three principal courses of action against the fianchetto. The first is to develop naturally with ♘c3, ♘f3, ♗e2 and 0-0 (Games 38-39), in the hope of maintaining a small plus with the central pawns. The second method entails an early c4-c5 (Games 40-41), after which White posts his pieces actively, intending a quick attack. The flip side of this is that c4-c5 is a committal pawn move which often allows Black to strike back with a timely ...b7-b6 or ...e7-e5. Lastly, White can flick in an early h2-h3 (Games 42-43), which has the merit of

preventing ...♗g4 ideas, but does allow Black time to arrange some alternative counterplay.

Later on in this chapter (Games 44-45) we shall look at lines with ...♗g4 (instead of ...g7-g6). Black's plan here is to continue development with ...e7-e6, ...♗e7, ...0-0 and ...♘c6. 4...♘f6 (Game 47) is extremely rare, but looks okay, especially if played in conjunction with ...♗g4.

> ### Game 38
> ### Brodsky-Maliutin
> *Moscow 1991*

1 e4 d5 2 exd5 ♘f6 3 d4 ♘xd5 4 c4 ♘b6 5 ♘f3 g6 6 ♗e2 ♗g7 7 ♘c3 0-0 8 0-0 ♘c6

This is Black's most challenging response here, immediately putting pressure on the white centre. The alternative 8...♗g4 will be scrutinised in Game 39.

9 d5!

This simple yet effective advance was popularised by Judit Polgar, who scored a crushing victory with it against 2...♘f6 expert Hannes Stefansson in 1988. It is certainly far superior to 9 ♗e3 which can be effectively met by 9...♗g4! One example continued 10 c5 ♘d5 11 ♘xd5 ♕xd5 12 h3 ♗f5 13 ♕a4 ♗e4 14 ♖ad1 ♕f5 15 ♖d2 ♖fd8 16 ♖fd1 h6 17 ♘e1 e6 18 ♗g4 ♕d5, and Black has at least equalised in Durban-O.Rodriguez, Benasque Open 1993.

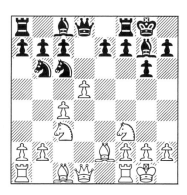

9...♘e5

Judit Polgar gives 9...♘a5 10 c5! ♗xc3 11 cxb6 ♗g7 12 ♗f4 ♗xb2 13 bxc7 as good for White, which cannot be argued with. In this line 12...axb6 13 b4 ♗xa1 14 ♕xa1 ♘b3 15 ♕b2! is also very strong, as the knight has nowhere to run.

10 c5!

A relatively new wrinkle. Against Stefansson, Polgar played the natural 10 ♘xe5 ♗xe5 11 ♗h6 and after 11...♗g7?! 12 ♗xg7 ♔xg7 13 ♕d4+ White's space advantage was notable. Since that encounter it has been shown that 11...♖e8! is a significant improvement, as it is beneficial for Black to retain his dark-squared bishop. After 12 ♕d2 e6 (12...c6 is also possible) Black has fair counter-chances. V.Ivanov-Maliutin, Moscow 1990, continued 13 ♖fe1 exd5 14 cxd5 ♗f5 15 ♖ad1 ♕h4 16 g3 ♕b4 17 a3

♕b3 18 ♖c1 ♖ad8 19 ♗d1 ♕c4 20 ♗g5 ♗xc3 21 ♖xc3 ♕xd5!, when the complications favoured Black.

10...♘xf3+ 11 ♗xf3 ♘d7 12 ♗e3 ♘e5 13 ♗e2 c6

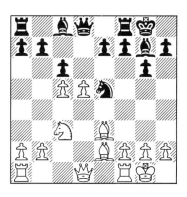

Perhaps Black could consider 13...b6 here. Magem Badals-Pomes, San Sebastian Open 1993, continued 14 ♖c1 bxc5 15 ♗xc5 ♗b7 16 ♕b3 ♘d7 17 ♗a3 ♘b6 18 ♖fd1 ♗e5 19 ♘b5 a6 20 ♕e3 ♘d7 21 ♘d4 ♗d6 22 ♘c6 ♗xc6 23 ♖xc6 ♘b6 24 ♗f3 ♕d7 25 h4 ♖fb8 26 h5 ♖b7 27 hxg6 hxg6 28 ♖d4 ♕f5 29 g3 and the players agreed a draw, although I suspect that White was a little better at some point.

14 f4! ♘d7 15 ♗f3 ♕a5?

Following this slip Black finds himself in tactically choppy waters. Brodsky gives two other possibilities:

a) 15...cxd5 16 ♕xd5 ♕a5 17 c6! with a clear plus.

b) 15...♕c7! is the best means of damage limitation, when 16 ♖c1 ♘f6 17 ♕e2 ♖d8 18 ♖fd1 is only slightly better for White.

16 dxc6 ♘xc5 17 ♘d5! ♗xb2 18 ♖b1 ♗g7 19 ♘xe7+ ♔h8 20 cxb7 ♗xb7 21 ♗xb7 ♖ae8 22 ♕d5 ♘xb7

23 ♖xb7 ♕c3 24 ♕c5

In the complications White has simply won a piece and consolidated. The contest is over.

24...♕d3 25 ♖xa7 ♖b8 26 ♘c6 ♖b5 27 ♕a3 ♕e4 28 ♖a8 ♔g8 29 ♘e7+ ♕xe7 30 ♕xe7 ♖xa8 31 ♖d1 ♖bb8 32 ♖d7 1-0

An important theoretical game. 10 c5! does seem to give White an edge.

Game 39
P.H.Nielsen-Mileto
Forli Open 1992

---

1 e4 d5 2 exd5 ♘f6 3 d4 ♘xd5 4 c4 ♘b6 5 ♘f3 g6 6 ♗e2 ♗g7 7 0-0 0-0 8 ♘c3 ♗g4

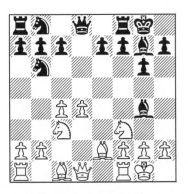

9 c5 ♘d5 10 ♕b3 ♘xc3 11 bxc3 b6 12 ♗a3 bxc5 13 ♗xc5 ♘d7 14 ♗a3 ♘b6 15 ♖ad1 c6 16 h3 ♗e6 17 c4 ♖b8 18 ♕c2

The influential pawns on c4 and d4, coupled with the fantastic bishop on a3, all add up to a large preference for the white pieces.

18...♖e8 19 ♗d3 ♗f6 20 ♖fe1 ♕d7 21 ♘e5

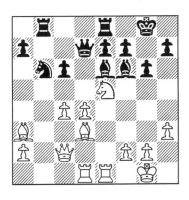

21...♗xe5?!

Good or bad, Black had to try 21...♕c8 here, as off-loading this bishop is equivalent to suicide.

22 ♖xe5 f6 23 ♖e3 ♗f5 24 ♗xf5 ♕xf5 25 ♕e2 ♖b7 26 ♗xe7 ♔f7 27 ♗c5 ♖xe3 28 ♕xe3! ♘xc4?

Falling into a neat trap, but Black

was busted in any case.

29 ♕h6 1-0

White is threatening to smoke out the king with ♕xh7+ or ♕f8+. After 29...g5 (what else?) 30 ♕f8+ ♔g6 31 ♕g8+ White picks up the stray knight on c4.

Game 40
Svidler-Yedidia
New York Open 1995

---

1 e4 d5 2 exd5 ♘f6 3 d4 ♘xd5 4 ♘f3 g6 5 c4 ♘b6

White often reaches this position via the 4 ♘f3 move order. 4 ♘f3 lines which exclude an early c2-c4 will be discussed in Chapter 7.

6 ♘c3 ♗g7 7 c5!?

This cunning move can be played either here or at move six. Black has to proceed with great care, as White often goes onto the offensive quite quickly.

7...♘d5!?

7...♘d5 seems to have replaced 7...♘6d7, which looks a bit too passive for my liking and hasn't scored well in tournament play. One fairly recent example went 8 ♗c4 0-0 9 0-0

♘c6 10 ♖e1 ♘f6 11 d5 ♘a5 12 ♗f1 c6 13 d6 exd6 14 b4 d5 15 bxa5 ♘e4 16 ♘xe4 dxe4 17 ♕xd8 ♖xd8 18 ♗g5 ♖d5 19 ♖ac1 ♗g4 20 ♗c4 ♖f5 21 ♗e3 exf3 22 h3!, and Black's bishop was trapped in Ulibin-Cuero, Ibercaja Open 1994. Of course Black has other options, but the general opinion is that White has a good position.

8 ♗c4 c6 9 ♕b3 0-0 10 0-0 ♘xc3 11 bxc3 b5 12 cxb6 axb6 13 ♖e1 b5

13...♗a6 is considered (by transposition) in the next game.

14 ♗d3 ♗e6?

15 ♖xe6!

I'm sure the young Russian GM didn't hesitate too long before lashing out with this. This type of sacrifice is meat and drink to players of Svidler's strength. Black's kingside pawn structure is blown to pieces.

15...fxe6 16 ♕xe6+ ♔h8 17 ♘g5 ♗xd4!?

A gallant attempt at counterplay which actually comes quite close to working. However, White has a brilliant refutation ready. After the submissive 17...♕e8, 18 ♕h3 does the trick, e.g. 18...h5 19 ♘e6 and the

white knight hits c7 and f8.
18 cxd4 ♕xd4 19 ♕e2!!

19...♕d6

A sad retreat, but 19...♕xa1 20
♕xe7 ♕xc1+ 21 ♗f1 leaves Black defenceless against the threats to h7 and
f8.
**20 ♗b2+ ♔g8 21 ♗c2 ♖d8 22 ♖d1
1-0**

A fantastic game from Svidler, although it has to be said that 14...♗e6
was a rather compliant move.

Game 41
M.Müller-Smagin
Germany 1992

**1 e4 d5 2 exd5 ♘f6 3 d4 ♘xd5 4 c4
♘b6 5 ♘f3 g6 6 c5 ♘d5 7 ♗c4 ♗g7
8 ♕b3 c6 9 ♘c3**

see following diagram

9...0-0!

Offering to sacrifice a pawn, although in reality 9...0-0 is Black's
only choice. 9...e6, blocking the light-squared bishop and creating a huge
hole on d6, just does not appeal.
10 0-0

Both 10 ♗xd5 cxd5 11 ♕xd5 ♘c6!?

and 10 ♘xd5 cxd5 11 ♗xd5 ♘c6 12
♗xc6 bxc6 offer Black good play for
the pawn. 10 0-0 leads the game back
into normal channels.

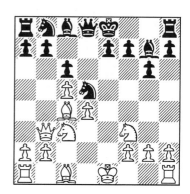

**10...♘xc3 11 bxc3 b5 12 cxb6
axb6 13 ♖e1**

After 13 ♖e1 we have actually
transposed back into Game 40.
Smagin's next move is an improvement over 13...b5.
**13...♗a6 14 ♗g5 ♗xc4 15 ♕xc4
♖e8 16 ♖ab1?!**

Here Smagin suggests 16 a4! as a
better idea. This move certainly does
have the merit of preventing Black's
following plan.
16...b5! 17 ♕b3 ♖a4!

A typical Scandinavian idea. Black
secures that all-important bind on
light squares.
**18 ♘e5 ♗xe5!? 19 dxe5 ♘a6 20
♖bd1 ♕c8 21 e6 f6!**

see following diagram

White's position looks quite impressive, but it actually cannot be improved upon. Meanwhile there is a
worthy outpost waiting for the black
knight on d5, while the e6-pawn simply turns out to be a weakness.

22 ♗e3 ♘c7 23 ♖d7 ♖c4!

Excluding the white queen from the real action. Black already has an edge.

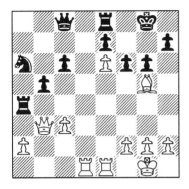

24 ♕a3 ♘d5 25 ♗d4 ♖a4 26 ♕c1 ♖d8

This keeps it all under control. 26...♖xa2 would have allowed White some irritating counterplay starting with 27 c4!

27 ♖xd8+ ♕xd8 28 h4 ♖c4 29 ♕a3 ♕c8 30 ♕a7 c5! 31 ♕d7 cxd4 32 ♕xd5 dxc3 33 ♕xb5 c2 34 ♖c1 ♕xe6 35 h5 gxh5 36 ♕xh5 ♕d6 37 g3 ♔g7 38 ♕e2 ♕c5 39 a4 h5 40 a5 h4 41 a6

Smagin gives 41 gxh4 ♖xh4 42 ♕e3 as White's last hope, but 42...♖g4+ 43 ♔f1 ♕c4+ 44 ♔e1 ♖e4 simply wins the queen.

41...hxg3 42 a7 ♕xf2+ 0-1

see following diagram

43 ♕xf2 gxf2+ 44 ♔xf2 ♖a4 45 ♖xc2 ♖xa7 leads to a trivial win. A model performance from Smagin. It seems that if Black can manage to obtain a fix on the light squares on the queenside, then most of his problems disappear.

Game 42
Hellers-J.Kristiansen
Gausdal 1987

1 e4 d5 2 exd5 ♘f6 3 d4 ♘xd5 4 ♘f3 g6 5 c4 ♘b6 6 h3

Generally speaking h2-h3 is always quite desirable, since it cuts out any annoying ...♗g4 pins. A tempo is a tempo, though, which does grant Black the opportunity to organise some serious counterplay involving an early ...e7-e5.

6...♗g7 7 ♘c3 0-0 8 ♗e3 ♘c6 9 ♕d2

This is the most menacing move here. After the pedestrian 9 ♗e2 e5 10

d5 ♘e7 11 0-0 Black plays 11...h6!, followed by ...♘f5, with good prospects.

9...e5 10 d5 ♘e7

See the next game for 10...♘a5.

11 g4 e4!?

11...f5 is Black's other principal option. Sometimes it simply transposes to 11...e4, but it also presents Black with other choices, as well as excluding White's chance to play 12 ♘xe4. So we can conclude that 11...f5 is at least more flexible, if not objectively stronger than 12...e4.

After 11...f5 12 0-0-0 Black can transpose into the main game with 12...e4 13 ♘g5 or try 12...fxg4!? 13 ♘g5 and now:

a) 13...g3!? 14 fxg3?! (Israeli IM Afek suggests 14 c5!? g2 15 ♗xg2 ♘c4 16 ♕e2 ♘xe3 17 fxe3 with an advantage to White) 14...♖xf1! 15 ♖hxf1 ♘xc4 16 ♕f2 and here Afek reckons Black has good chances after 16...♘f5! 17 ♗d2 ♘xd2 18 ♕xd2 ♘d4.

b) 13...♘f5 14 hxg4 ♘xe3 15 ♕xe3 ♖f4 16 ♘e6 ♗xe6 17 dxe6 and White's light-square control ensured a clear edge in Cao-Peredy, Budapest 1996.

12 ♘g5

On 12 ♘xe4 comes 12...f5! 13 ♘c5 fxg4 14 ♘g5 ♘f5 15 ♘ge6 ♗xe6 16 ♘xe6 ♕f6!, and Black's control of the a1-h8 diagonal gives rise to an extremely messy position. My own feeling is that White should be better, but I am not sure if I would like to prove it in a practical game!

12...f5 13 0-0-0 h6

Not 13...♗h6? 14 ♘e6 ♗xe3 15 ♕xe3 ♗xe6 16 dxe6 ♕c8 17 c5, as the knight on b6 has no squares.

14 ♘e6 ♗xe6 15 dxe6 ♕xd2+ 16 ♖xd2 ♖fd8 17 ♖xd8+ ♖xd8

18 c5! ♘bd5 19 ♘xd5 ♘xd5 20 ♗c4 ♔f8 21 ♖d1 c6 22 gxf5 gxf5 23 ♖g1 ♗f6 24 ♗xh6+ ♔e7 25 ♖g6 ♖h8 26 ♔d1 ♖h7 27 a3

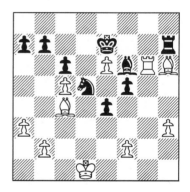

27...a5

Naturally Black would really like to remove the e6-pawn, but 27...♔xe6 allows a won king and pawn endgame after 28 ♗xd5+ cxd5 29 ♗g5 ♖f7 30 b4 ♔e5 31 ♗xf6+ ♖xf6 32 ♖xf6 ♔xf6 33 b5 d4 34 h4 d3 35 c6 bxc6 36 bxc6 ♔e6 37 h5!, and one of the pawns will promote.

28 b3 ♘c3+ 29 ♔e1 a4 30 b4 ♘d5 31 b5 ♖h8 32 b6! ♖d8 33 ♗g7 ♗h4

The advanced b-pawn makes its presence felt. Black has to allow infiltration, as 33...♗xg7 34 ♖xg7+ ♔xe6 35 ♖xb7 is terminal.

34 ♗e5 e3 35 ♗d6+ ♖xd6 36 cxd6+ ♔xd6 37 ♗xd5 cxd5 38 ♔e2 ♗xf2 39 ♖g7 ♔xe6 40 ♖xb7 d4 41 ♖g7 1-0

The only way to stop the b-pawn is by 41...d3+ 42 ♔xd3 e2 43 ♔xe2 ♗xb6, but this runs into 44 ♖g6+ and 45 ♖xb6. An energetic game from Hellers, who never allowed Black to consolidate his position.

Game 43
Papatheodorou-Thorhallsson
Katerini 1993

---

1 e4 d5 2 exd5 ♘f6 3 d4 ♘xd5 4 c4 ♘b6 5 ♘c3 g6 6 ♗e3 ♗g7 7 h3 0-0 8 ♘f3 ♘c6 9 ♕d2 e5 10 d5 ♘a5!?

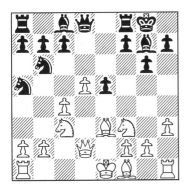

This move has become more common recently and it has proved to be quite problematical for White, who has no visible route to an advantage.

11 b3 f5 12 ♗h6

There are two other options here, one good, one not so good:

a) 12 ♗c5 ♖e8 and now:

a1) 13 0-0-0! ♘d7 14 ♗b4 c5 15 ♗xa5 ♕xa5 16 ♘b5 ♕d8 17 ♘d6 ♖f8 18 ♘g5 ♗h6 19 h4 e4 20 ♘xc8 ♖xc8 21 ♔c2 ♗xg5!? 22 hxg5 f4 23 ♖e1 (23 g3 e3! 24 fxe3 fxg3 25 e4 ♖f2 26 ♗e2 ♘e5 is better for Black) 23...♕e7 24 g3 fxg3 25 f4! ♖ce8 26 ♕e3 ♖f7 27 ♗h3 ♘f8 28 ♖hg1 ♕c7 29 ♖ef1 b5 with a very messy position in Malev-Malinin, Correspondence 1990-92.

a2) 13 ♗e2 ♘d7 14 ♗a3 c5 15 ♘g5 ♗h6 16 h4 b6 17 ♗b2 ♘f8 18 f4 exf4 19 ♕xf4 ♘b7 20 ♘b5 ♕e7 21 ♕d2 a6 22 ♘c3 ♘d6 23 0-0-0 ♗d7 24 ♖he1 ♕e3 25 ♘f3 b5 with a black initiative in St.Nikolic-Stefansson, Komotini 1993.

b) 12 0-0-0?! e4 13 ♘e1 ♕f6 14 ♔b2 c6 15 d6 ♗e6 16 ♘c2 ♘axc4+ and Black has just won a pawn as 17 bxc4 allows 17...♘a4+, while 17 ♗xc4 ♗xc4 is also strong, Markovic-Gostovic, Yugoslavia 1985.

12...e4 13 ♗xg7 ♔xg7 14 ♘d4 c5!

Black has to retort quickly on the queenside, otherwise he may just end up with a lifeless position.

15 ♘c2

The alternative is to simplify with 15 dxc6, which led to an balanced position after 15...♘xc6 16 0-0-0 ♕f6 17 ♘xc6 bxc6 18 ♕d4 ♗e6 19 ♕xf6+ ♔xf6 20 f4 exf3 21 gxf3 ♖fd8 in Suetin-Smagin, USSR 1984.

15...♘d7 16 0-0-0 ♘e5 17 ♗e2 b6!

see following diagram

It is well known that knights are excellent blockaders of passed pawns. Here Black plans ...♘a5-b7-d6, when both black knights would be admirably posted.

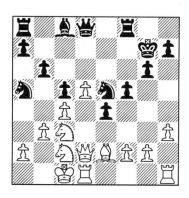

18 g4 ♘b7 19 h4 ♘d6 20 ♕f4?

I do not understand this move, which just gives up a pawn for no particular reason. I prefer 20 gxf5 with a roughly level position.

20...♘xg4 21 ♗xg4 fxg4 22 ♕e5+ ♕f6 23 ♕xf6+ ♖xf6 24 ♖d2 ♗d7 25 ♖e1 ♖e8 26 ♖de2 ♖f4 27 ♘e3 ♖f3 28 ♔b2 h5 29 ♘g2 ♔h6 0-1

Perhaps the resignation was premature, but White's suffering would be drawn out in this hopeless endgame.

> ### Game 44
> ### R.Byrne-Rogoff
> *USA Championship 1978*

1 e4 d5 2 exd5 ♘f6 3 d4 ♘xd5 4 c4

♘b6 5 ♘f3 ♗g4 6 c5

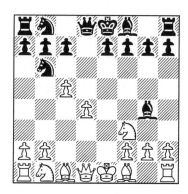

The most daring try against 5...♗g4. 6 ♗e2 will be examined in Game 45.

6...♘6d7

Black has to be careful as other moves fall short of the mark:

a) 6...♘d5 7 ♕b3! and now:

a1) 7...♗xf3 8 ♕xb7! ♘e3 9 ♕xf3 ♘c2+ 10 ♔d1 ♘xa1 11 ♗b5+ (or 11 ♕xa8) 11...♘d7 12 ♗xd7+ ♔xd7 13 ♕d5+ ♔e8 14 ♕c6+ ♕d7 15 ♕xa8+ ♕d8 16 ♕xd8+ ♔xd8 17 b3 e5 18 ♗b2 and Black resigned in Von Herman-Jentsch, Germany 1992.

a2) 7...♗c8 8 ♘c3 e6 9 ♘xd5 exd5 10 ♗f4 ♗e7 11 ♗d3 0-0 12 0-0 ♘c6 13 h3 ♗f6 14 ♕c3 a5 15 ♖fe1 ♗e6 16 ♖e2 ♕d7 17 ♖ae1 ♖fc8 18 ♗b5 ♗f5 19 ♗e5 ♕d8 20 ♗xc6 bxc6 21 ♗xf6 ♕xf6 22 ♘e5 and the white knight is a monster, Y.Grünfeld-Afek, Israel 1986.

b) 6...♗xf3 7 ♕xf3 ♘d5 8 ♕b3 b6 9 ♗g5 ♕d7 10 ♘c3 e6 11 ♘xd5 ♕xd5 12 ♕xd5 exd5 13 c6 and Black's queenside is permanently sealed, Suetin-Shamkovich, USSR Championship 1964.

7 ♗c4

7 h3!? may possibly be the most accurate move-order. After 7...♗xf3 8 ♕xf3 ♘c6 9 ♗e3 e5 10 dxe5 ♘dxe5 11 ♕e4 ♕d7 12 ♘c3 f5 13 ♕a4 0-0-0 14 ♖d1 ♕e8 15 ♗e2 ♖xd1+ 16 ♕xd1 f4 17 ♗xf4 ♗xc5 18 0-0 ♖f8 19 ♗h2 ♕g6 20 ♕d5 White's bishop pair in an open position was enough for an edge in Illescas Cordoba-Corbin, Novi Sad Olympiad 1990. Naturally Black can play 7...♗h5, but after 8 ♗c4 e6 (8...♘c6!?) 9 ♗e3 we reach the game position without Black having the option discussed in the note to his eighth move.

7...e6

7...♘c6? runs into 8 ♗xf7+! ♔xf7 9 ♘g5+ and 10 ♕xg4.

8 h3 ♗h5

8...♗xf3!? is a promising alternative. Following 9 ♕xf3 ♘c6 10 ♗e3 ♕f6 11 ♘c3!? ♕xf3 12 gxf3 0-0-0 13 0-0-0 ♗e7 14 a3 e5 15 d5 ♘d4 16 b4 ♘xf3 17 ♘b5 a6 18 ♘xc7 ♔xc7 19 d6+ ♗xd6 20 cxd6+ ♔b8 21 ♗xf7 ♖hf8 22 ♗d5 ♘d4 23 ♔b2 ♘f6 24 ♗g2 ♘e8 25 f4 ♘xd6 26 ♗xd4 exd4 27 ♖xd4 ♘f5 the players agreed a draw in Tischbierek-Grottke, Zittau 1989. But White can play 7 h3!? ♗h5 8 ♗c4 e6 if he wants to reach the game position.

9 ♗e3 ♘c6 10 ♘c3 ♗e7 11 a3 e5 12 d5 ♘d4 13 g4! ♘xf3+ 14 ♕xf3 ♗g6 15 b4

see following diagram

15...0-0?!

Lunging with 15...e4!? is critical here, as 16 ♘xe4? loses to 16...♘e5.

16 ♖d1 e4 17 ♕f4 ♖e8 18 ♘b5! ♖c8 19 d6 cxd6 20 ♘xd6 ♗xd6 21

♖xd6

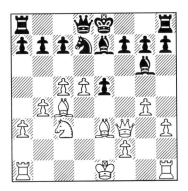

The rook does a magnificent job on d6, supported by White's queenside pawn phalanx. Likewise the bishop on c4 is also impressively posted. All this adds up to a decisive advantage for White.

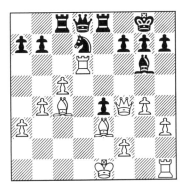

21...♕e7 22 ♗d4 ♖c6 23 h4 e3

This desperate pawn sacrifice is an attempt to relieve some of the intolerable pressure, but perhaps Black should have tried to 'grin and bear it' with 23...h6.

24 fxe3 ♖xd6 25 cxd6 ♕e4 26 0-0 ♕xf4 27 ♖xf4 h5 28 gxh5 ♗xh5 29 ♖f5 ♗g6 30 ♖g5! ♖c8 31 ♖xg6 1-0

31...♖xc4 32 ♖xg7+ ♔f8 33 ♖h7 is the end.

Game 45
Penrose-Goldenberg
Correspondence 1991

1 e4 d5 2 exd5 ♘f6 3 d4 ♘xd5 4 ♘f3 ♗g4 5 c4 ♘b6 6 ♗e2 ♘c6

This discourages ♘e5 ideas, but Black should consider delaying ...♘c6, in order to cut out the dangerous 9 d5. After 6...e6 7 0-0 ♗e7 we have reached, by transposition, the game J.Polgar-Kamsky, Monaco 1995, which continued 8 ♘c3 0-0 9 h3 ♗xf3 10 ♗xf3 ♘c6 11 c5 ♘d5 12 ♘xd5 exd5 13 ♗e3 ♗f6 14 ♕d3 g6, and Black had equalised.

7 0-0 e6 8 ♘c3 ♗e7 9 d5 exd5 10 cxd5 ♘b4 11 ♕d4!

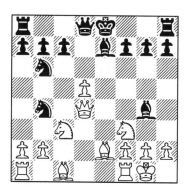

11...♗xf3 12 ♕xg7!?

This leads to fantastic complications, which seem to favour White. The other major choice is 12 ♗xf3 and then:

a) 12...♘c2? 13 ♕xg7 ♗f6 14 ♕g4 ♘xa1 15 ♖e1+ ♗e7 16 ♗g5 ♘c8 (16...♖g8 17 ♗xe7! ♖xg4 18 ♗c5+ ♔d7 19 ♗xg4+ wins) 17 d6! cxd6 18 ♗xb7 and Black is busted.

b) 12...0-0 13 ♕d1 ♘c4 14 ♖e1 ♖e8

15 a3 ♘a6 16 ♗e2 ♘d6 17 ♕c2 ♗f6 18 ♗e3 and White's comfortable space advantage gives him a small edge, Lau-S.Bücker, Germany 1994.

12...♗f6 13 ♗b5+ c6 14 ♖e1+ ♔d7 15 dxc6+ bxc6 16 ♕g3!

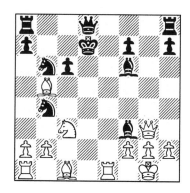

16...♗xc3

In his notes to the game Polish Master Przewoznik gives 16...cxb5 17 ♕h3+! and:

a) 17...♔c6 18 ♕xf3+ ♔c7 19 ♕f4+ and ♕xb4. Przewoznik does not mention the improved defence 18...♘4d5, but 19 ♘xd5 ♘xd5 20 ♗h6! ♗xb2 21 ♖ad1 ♖g8 22 ♖e2 ♗c3 23 ♖e3! (*Fritz*) 23...♗b4 24 ♖e5! seems to win.

b) 17...♔c7 18 ♗f4+ ♔b7 19 ♕xf3+ ♔a6 20 a4! with a tremendous attack.

17 bxc3 cxb5 18 ♗g5 f6 19 ♕xf3 ♘4d5 20 ♗e3 ♔c7 21 ♖ad1 ♖e8 22 a4!

Not 22 ♗xb6+ ♘xb6! and White's back rank is weak. Now the decisive 23 a5 is threatened and 22...bxa4 loses to 23 c4.

22...♕d6 23 a5 ♖ed8 24 axb6+ axb6 25 g3

White has regained the piece and Black is still in total disarray. The rest is easy.

25...♕c6 26 ♗f4+ ♔b7 27 ♖d3 ♖d7 28 ♖ed1 ♖ad8 29 h4 h5 30 ♕e4 ♔c8 31 ♖d4 ♔b7 32 ♔h2 ♕c5 33 ♕f5 ♕c6 34 ♖4d2 ♕c4 35 ♕xh5 ♕e4 36 ♕g4 f5 37 ♕g6 ♘xf4 38 ♖xd7+ ♖xd7 39 ♖xd7+ ♔c8

40 ♖d8+! ♔xd8 41 ♕d6+ ♔c8 42 ♕xf4 ♕e6 43 h5 1-0

> ### Game 46
> ### Velicka-B.Lalic
> *Vera Menchik Memorial 1994*

1 e4 d5 2 exd5 ♘f6 3 d4 ♘xd5 4 c4 ♘b6 5 ♘c3 e5!

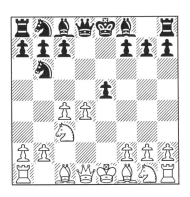

6 d5

Other moves are:

a) 6 ♘f3 exd4 7 ♘xd4 ♗e7 8 ♗e2

0-0 9 0-0 ♗d7 10 ♗e3 ♘a6 11 ♕c2 ♘b4 12 ♕b1 ♗g5 and Black was fine in I.Zaitsev-Maliutin, Minsk 1993.

b) 6 dxe5 ♕xd1+ 7 ♘xd1 ♘c6 8 ♘f3 ♗g4 9 ♗e2 0-0-0 10 ♗g5 ♖e8 11 ♘e3 ♗xf3 12 gxf3 ♗b4+ 13 ♔f1 ♘xe5 and again Black has no worries, Afek-Veinger, Israel 1986.

6...c6 7 ♗e3

This introduces a forcing line, the consequences of which are not unfavourable for Black.

7...cxd5 8 c5 d4 9 cxb6 dxe3 10 ♕xd8+ ♔xd8 11 bxa7 exf2+ 12 ♔xf2 ♗c5+ 13 ♔g3 ♘c6 14 ♘f3 f5 15 ♖d1+ ♔e7 16 ♘d5+ ♔f8 17 h4 ♖xa7

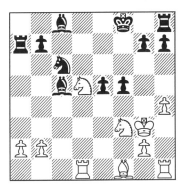

I like the look of Black's position here, with the impressive pawn front on e5 and f5, complimented by the two bishops. The only uncertainty remains the brief inactivity of the rook on h8, and White uses this to muddy the waters enough to obtain a draw.

18 b4 f4+ 19 ♔h2 ♗f2 20 b5 ♘d4 21 ♘xe5 ♗g3+ 22 ♔g1 ♖xa2 23 ♗c4 ♖b2 24 ♗d3 ♗e6 25 ♘xf4! ♗xf4 26 ♖f1 ♘e2+ 27 ♗xe2 ♖xe2 28 ♖xf4+ ♔e7 29 ♘f3 ♗d5 30 ♖f5

♗e4 31 ♖e5+ ♔d6 32 ♔f1 ♗xf3 33 ♖xe2 ♗xe2+ 34 ♔xe2 ♖e8+ 35 ♔d3 ♖e6

I have a token preference for Black in this endgame, due to White's weak b5-pawn, but with best play it is a draw.

36 ♖c1 ♖g6 37 b6 ♖xg2 38 ♖c7 h5 39 ♔e3 ♖g4 40 ♖xb7 ♔c6 41 ♖f7 ♔xb6 42 ♖f5 ♖xh4 43 ♖g5 ½-½

43...♖g4 44 ♖xg4 hxg4 45 ♔f4 is a stone dead draw. It seems that 5...e5! is a complete answer to 5 ♘c3.

Game 47
M.Pribyl-Klaschus
Pardubice Open 1992

---

1 e4 d5 2 exd5 ♘f6 3 d4 ♘xd5 4 ♘f3 ♘f6 5 ♗e2 ♗g4 6 0-0 e6 7 c4

Via a very unusual move-order we have arrived at the variation 1 e4 d5 2 exd5 ♘f6 3 d4 ♘xd5 4 c4 ♘f6!? (instead of 4...♘b6) 5 ♘f3 ♗g4 6 ♗e2 e6 7 0-0.

7...♗e7 8 ♘c3 0-0 9 ♗e3

see following diagram

9...c6

This is very solid, but possibly too

committal. After the flexible 9...♘bd7 10 ♘e5 ♗xe2 11 ♕xe2 Black has the choice of playing 11...c5, which would save a tempo over the game.

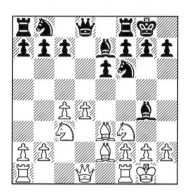

Now White gradually builds up a menacing offensive against the black king.

10 h3 ♗h5 11 ♘e5 ♗xe2 12 ♕xe2 ♘bd7 13 f4 c5 14 ♖ad1 cxd4 15 ♗xd4 ♕c8 16 ♘xd7 ♘xd7 17 f5! e5

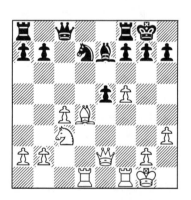

18 ♘d5! ♗c5 19 ♗xc5 ♕xc5+ 20 ♔h1 ♘b6 21 f6 ♘xd5 22 ♖xd5 ♕c7 23 ♖xe5 1-0

I suppose that Black could have struggled on for a while, but there is something to be said for reserving one's energy in positions such as this one.

Summary

The ...g7-g6 system continues to be a tough nut to crack for White. Simple development as in Brodsky-Maliutin (Game 38) offers White the chance of a small edge, while the well prepared Black player has enough resources against the more ambitious h2-h3 and c4-c5 lines. White has scored quite well against the ...♗g4 lines, but the fact that grandmasters such as Gata Kamsky and Bogdan Lalic have utilised it to good effect should give encouragement to the Black player.

1 e4 d5 2 exd5 ♘f6 3 d4 ♘xd5 4 c4
4...♘b6
> 4...♘f6 5 ♘f3 ♗g4 6 ♗e2 e6 7 0-0 - *game 47*

5 ♘f3 *(D)*
> 5 ♘c3 - *game 46*

5...g6
> 5...♗g4 *(D)*
>> 6 c5 - *game 44*
>> 6 ♗e2 - *game 45*

6 ♗e2
> 6 ♘c3 ♗g7 7 c5 ♘d5 8 ♗c4 c6 9 ♕b3 0-0 10 0-0 ♘xc3 11 bxc3 b5
> 12 cxb6 axb6 13 ♖e1
>> 13...b5 - *game 40*
>> 13...♗a6 - *game 41*
> 6 h3 ♗g7 7 ♘c3 0-0 8 ♗e3 ♘c6 9 ♕d2 e5 10 d5
>> 10...♘e7 - *game 42*
>> 10...♘a5 - *game 43*

6...♗g7 7 ♘c3 0-0 8 0-0 *(D)*
> 8...♘c6 - *game 38*
> 8...♗g4 - *game 39*

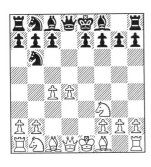
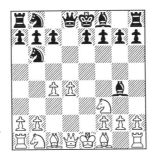
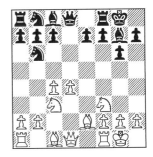

| 5 ♘f3 | 5...♗g4 | 8 0-0 |

CHAPTER SEVEN

2...♘f6: Main Line without c2-c4

1 e4 d5 2 exd5 ♘f6 3 d4 ♘xd5 4 ♘f3

After 3 d4 ♘xd5 4 ♘f3 White often plays an early c2-c4, which generally transposes to variations considered in Chapter 6. In this chapter we shall instead examine lines in which White delays or does without c2-c4.

Black's most common choice of action is to develop with ...g7-g6, ...♗g7 and ...0-0. He must then decide whether to attack White's centre immediately with a swift ...c7-c5, or to play more solidly with ...c7-c6. An early ...c7-c5 has been a favourite of the Icelandic GM Hannes Stefansson and it often involves a speculative pawn sacrifice (see Games 48 and 50). The big question usually revolves around whether White is able to hold on to the extra pawn. With the more restrained ...c7-c6 (Game 49) Black decides to coordinate his forces further before striking out in the centre.

5 ♗c4, applying pressure on f7, is White's only real alternative to 5 ♗e2. Once again Black has a choice of pawn breaks in the centre. Game 51 sees an early ...c7-c5, while ...♗g4 followed by ...e7-e5 (Game 52) also deserves attention.

Finally we focus on 4...♗g4. Kicking the bishop with 5 h3 ♗h5 6 g4 (Game 53) usually leads to sharp play, where Black has a fair share of the action. Meanwhile the quiet 5 ♗e2 (Game 54), especially when followed by the plan of an early ♘e5, has been scoring well for White recently.

Game 48
Campora-Maliutin
Candas Open 1992

1 e4 d5 2 exd5 ♘f6 3 d4 ♘xd5 4 ♘f3 g6 5 ♗e2 ♗g7 6 0-0 0-0 7 ♖e1 c5!?

7...c5 is an ambitious attempt to disrupt the centre, before White has a chance to consolidate. 7...c6 will be studied in Game 49.

8 dxc5 ♘a6 9 ♗xa6 bxa6

We have reached a finely poised position. If Black is able to recapture the c5-pawn, then he will have an advantage due to the bishop pair and the open lines on which they can operate. On the other hand, if White retains the c5-pawn, then Black's compensation may be insignificant, and the pawn itself may prove to be a strength.

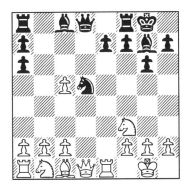

10 ♘bd2

Surprisingly this was a new move at the time, as the idea of ♘b1-d2-b3 does seem to suggest itself. Two previous tries had only yielded half a point for White:

a) 10 ♘e5 ♗e6 11 ♘d2 ♕c7 12 ♘d3 ♖fd8 13 ♕f3 ♗f5 14 ♘e4 ♖ac8 15 ♗g5 ♕c6 16 c4 ♘f6 17 ♘b4 ♕a4 18 ♗xf6 exf6 19 ♘d5 ♗xe4 20 ♕xe4 f5 21 ♘e7+ ♔h8 22 ♕h4 ♖a8 23 c6 ♕a5 24 ♕g3 ♗xb2 25 ♖ab1 ♗f6 26 c7 ♖e8 27 ♕d6 ♔g7 28 ♔f1 ♕xa2! 29 c8♕ ♖axc8 30 ♘xc8 ♕xc4+ 31 ♔g1 ♖xc8 32 h3 ♖c6 33 ♕a3 ♕f4 34 ♕d3 ♕d6 35 ♕xd6 ♖xd6 and the game was eventually drawn, Dolmatov-Vidarsson, Akureyri 1988.

b) 10 c3?! ♗b7 11 ♘d4 ♕c7 12 c6 ♗c8! (12...♗xc6 13 ♘xc6 ♕xc6 is also fine for Black, but 12...♗c8 looks for more) 13 ♕f3 ♖d8 14 ♘d2 e5 15 ♘c2 ♕xc6 16 c4 ♘e7 17 ♕xc6 ♘xc6 and, with the pawn safely recaptured, Black has reached an ideal position, Lobron-Stefansson, Moscow 1989.

10...♕c7 11 ♘b3 ♗b7 12 ♖b1 e5 13 ♗d2 ♖ae8 14 c4 ♘e7 15 ♗a5! ♕b8

After 15...♕c6, 16 ♗c3 gains time

as ♘a5 is threatened.

16 ♗c3 ♘c6 17 ♘bd2 f5 18 b4!

A critical position has been reached. Black would like to play in the centre with the natural 18...e4, but after 19 ♗xg7 ♔xg7 20 b5! Black cannot play 20...exf3 as 21 bxc6 wins for White. Therefore the black knight is forced to retreat, allowing the white knight a useful square in the centre.

18...♘d4

Now the position becomes more simplified and White's extra pawn starts to look very threatening.

19 b5 ♘xf3+ 20 ♘xf3 ♖d8 21 ♕b3! ♗xf3 22 gxf3 ♖d3 23 ♖bd1 ♖fd8

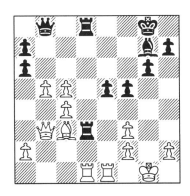

Capturing the f-pawn with 23...♖xf3 runs into 24 c6! e4 25 c5+

when all variations win for White:

a) 25...♖f7 26 ♖d7 and wins.

b) 25...♔h8 26 ♗xg7+ ♔xg7 27 ♖d7+ ♔h6 28 ♕b2! axb5 29 c7 ♕c8 30 ♕g7+ ♔g5 31 ♖d8 ♖xd8 32 ♕e7+ and 33 cxd8♕.

24 c6 e4 25 c5+ ♔f8 26 ♖xd3 ♖xd3 27 ♗xg7+ ♔xg7 28 ♕b2+ ♔f7 29 fxe4 axb5 30 e5 ♔e6 31 c7 ♕xc7 32 ♕xb5

The smoke has cleared, leaving White a clear pawn up. Meanwhile Black's king is by far the weaker of the two. The end is not long in coming.

32...♖d8 33 ♕c4+ ♔e7 34 e6 ♕a5 35 ♖e2 ♖d2 36 ♕h4+ ♔e8 37 ♕xh7 1-0

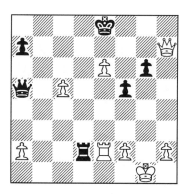

37...♖xe2 38 ♕f7+ ♔d8 39 ♕d7 is mate.

Game 49
Hebden-Hodgson
London (Lloyds Bank Masters) 1991

---

1 e4 d5 2 exd5 ♘f6 3 d4 ♘xd5 4 ♘f3 g6 5 ♗e2 ♗g7 6 0-0 0-0 7 ♖e1 c6 8 ♘a3

A characteristic idea in this position. The knight heads for c4, with-

out impeding the path of the bishop on c1.

8...♕c7 9 c3 ♘d7 10 ♘c4 c5

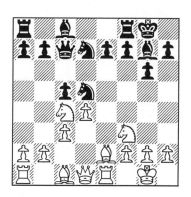

Black finally breaks with the c-pawn, now that it has the full support of his other pieces.

11 ♗f1 cxd4 12 ♘xd4 ♘7f6 13 ♘e5 ♖d8 14 ♕f3 a6 15 g4!? e6 16 ♗g5 b5 17 ♗g2 ♗b7 18 a4!

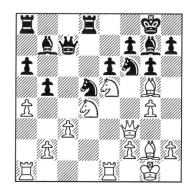

This is the only way to unsettle Black, who is very close to cementing into a good position.

18...♖ab8

After 18...♕b6 I am sure Hebden that was planning 19 ♘xf7! ♔xf7 20 ♖xe6, when Black's position starts to creak, e.g. 20...♖d6 21 ♗xf6 ♗xf6 22 ♖xd6 ♕xd6 23 g5. Meanwhile

18...bxa4 allows 19 c4.

19 axb5 axb5 20 ♘xb5 ♕c5 21 c4?

21 ♘d4! secures White's extra pawn, as 21...♘xc3 fails tactically to 22 ♕xc3 ♕xd4 23 ♕xd4 ♖xd4 24 ♗xb7 ♖xb7 25 ♖a8+ ♗f8 26 ♗h6!

21...h6 22 ♗e3 ♘xe3 23 ♕xe3 ♕xe3 24 ♖xe3 ♗xg2 25 ♔xg2

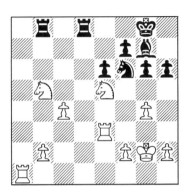

25...♘d5!

I guess that Hebden must have missed this shot, which virtually turns the tables.

26 cxd5 ♗xe5 27 ♘a7 ♗d4?

This is enough for equality, but what about 27...♗xb2! 28 ♖b1 ♖xd5, when Black is just a clear pawn up? Both 29 ♘c6 ♖b7 30 ♖e2 ♖db5 and 29 ♖e2 ♗e5 do nothing to rectify White's situation.

28 ♖f3 ♖xd5 29 ♘c6 ♖b7 30 ♖a8+ ♔g7 31 b4 ♗f6 32 ♖fa3 ♖d6 33 ♖3a6 ♖d2 34 ♖a2 ♖d3 35 ♖c2 ♖b5 36 ♖a7 h5 37 h3 hxg4 38 hxg4 ♖g5 39 ♖c4 ♖d2 40 ♖a5 ♖xa5 41 bxa5 ♗h4 42 ♖a4 ♗xf2 43 a6 g5 44 ♔f3 f5 ½-½

After 45 a7 ♗xa7 46 ♖xa7+ ♔f6 a draw is the only result. A fascinating struggle between the two English grandmasters.

> *Game 50*
> **Z.Horvath-Stefansson**
> *Budapest 1991*

1 e4 d5 2 exd5 ♘f6 3 d4 ♘xd5 4 ♘f3 g6 5 ♗e2 ♗g7 6 0-0 0-0 7 h3

Another approach is 7 ♘a3. In Juarez-Sariego, Sagua la Grande 1987, Black reaped the rewards of some adventurous play after 7...a5! 8 ♘c4 a4 9 ♗d2 c5! 10 dxc5 ♕c7 11 ♕c1 ♕xc5! 12 ♗h6 ♘c6 13 ♖d1 ♖d8 14 ♗xg7 ♔xg7, when Black was in command.

7...c5!?

This leads to play very similar to Game 48. Quieter moves such as 7...c6 are of course fully playable.

8 dxc5 ♘a6 9 ♗xa6 bxa6

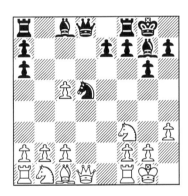

10 c4?!

After this move Black's pieces become increasingly active. I prefer 10 ♘bd2, in the style of Campora, although it has to be said that in comparison to Game 48, h2-h3 is less useful than ♖e1.

10...♘b4 11 ♘c3 ♗f5 12 ♘e1 ♕xd1 13 ♘xd1 ♖ac8 14 ♗e3 ♗e6 15 a3 ♘c6 16 ♘f3

The spare pawn cannot be saved, as

16 ♖c1 runs into 16...♘a5.

16...♗xc4

As discussed earlier, if Black is able to regain the sacrificed pawn, then he invariably ends up with an excellent position. Here, with the bishops raking across the open board, is no exception.

17 ♖e1 ♗d5 18 ♘d2 f5 19 f3 ♖fd8 20 ♖c1 a5! 21 ♘c3 ♗f7 22 ♘a4 ♖d3 23 ♘c4 ♖cd8 24 ♔f1 ♗f6! 25 ♖c2 ♘d4 26 ♗xd4 ♖8xd4

The bishops totally dominate the knights. In fact there is nothing to be done about the decisive threat of ...♗e8, winning a pawn.

27 ♖ec1 ♗e8 28 b3 ♖xb3 29 ♘ab2 ♖d5! 0-1

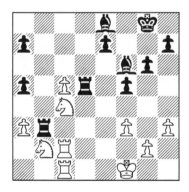

Black was threatening ...♗b5 and ...♖xc5. Another impressive performance from Stefansson.

Game 51
Rausis-Thorhallsson
Cappelle la Grande Open 1993

---

1 e4 d5 2 exd5 ♘f6 3 d4 ♘xd5 4 ♘f3 g6 5 ♗c4 ♗g7 6 0-0

Should White wish to avoid the early ...c7-c5 plan, then perhaps 6 c3 should be tried, as after 6 c3 ♘b6 7 ♗b3 c5 8 dxc5 ♕xd1+ 9 ♔xd1 ♘6d7 10 ♗e3 ♘a6 11 ♗a4 0-0 12 ♗xd7 ♗xd7 13 ♘bd2 Black is unable to regain the material.

6...♘b6

For 6...0-0 see the next game.

7 ♗b3 c5

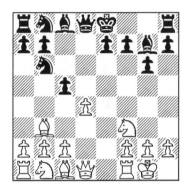

8 dxc5 ♕xd1 9 ♖xd1 ♘6d7 10 ♘c3 ♗xc3 11 bxc3 ♘xc5 12 ♗e3

An improvement over 12 ♘e5 ♘xb3 13 cxb3 f6 14 ♘d3 ♘c6 15 ♗e3 ♗f5 16 ♘c5 b6, when Black was fine and even went on to win in Tisch-bierek-Stefansson, Copenhagen 1991.

12...♘xb3 13 axb3 a6 14 ♗c5 ♘c6 15 ♘d4 ♗d7 16 ♖e1 0-0 17 ♘xc6 ♗xc6 18 ♗xe7

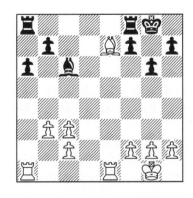

So White has won a pawn, but the opposite-coloured bishops make the winning task virtually impossible.

18...♖fe8 19 f3 ♔g7 20 ♔f2 ♖ac8 21 c4 ♖c7 22 ♗d6 ♖xe1 23 ♖xe1 ♖c8 24 ♗e5+ f6 25 ♗d4 ♔f7 26 c3 h5 27 h4 ♗d7 28 ♖a1 ♗f5 29 ♖a4 ♗d3 30 ♗e3 ♖c7 31 c5 ♗b5 32 ♖b4 ♖d7 33 ♗d4 ♖e7 34 c4 ♗c6 35 ♖b6 ♖d7 36 ♔e3 ♖e7+ 37 ♔f2 ♖d7 38 ♔e3 ♖e7+ 39 ♔d2 ♖d7 40 ♔d3 a5!

Preventing b3-b4-b5. In an attempt to make progress, White has incarcerated his own rook. The only way to free it would be with b3-b4, but this would allow an exchange and leave White with a inconsequential extra pawn.

41 ♔e3 ♖d8 42 ♗c3 ♖a8 43 ♔f4 ♔e6 44 g4 ♖a7 45 g5 f5 46 ♔e3 f4+! 47 ♔xf4 ♖a8 48 ♗f6 ♖a7 49 ♗e5 ♖a8 50 ♗d6 ♖a7 51 ♗c7 ♔d7 52 ♗e5 ♔e6 53 ♗c3 ♖a8 54 ♗g7 ♖d8 55 ♔e3 ♔f5 56 ♗c3 ♖e8+ 57 ♔f2 ♖a8 58 ♔g3 ♖a7 59 ♔f2 ♖a8 60 ♔g3 ♖a7 61 ♔f2 ♖a8 62 ♔e3 ♖e8+ 63 ♔f2 ½-½

Even two pawns up, it is apparent that White can make no further progress.

Game 52
Cao-Palkovi
Budapest 1995

---

1 e4 d5 2 exd5 ♘f6 3 d4 ♘xd5 4 ♘f3 g6 5 ♗c4 ♗g7 6 0-0 0-0 7 ♖e1 ♘b6 8 ♗b3 ♘c6 9 c3 ♗g4 10 ♗f4

In Morozevich-Comas, Pamplona 1995, the young Russian talent played the natural 10 h3, and after 10...♗xf3

11 ♕xf3 e5 12 dxe5 ♘xe5? (I don't understand this move at all) 13 ♕xb7 a5 14 ♘a3 a4 15 ♗c2 ♖b8 16 ♕a6 ♖a8 17 ♕e2 c6 18 ♗f4 ♖e8 19 ♖ad1 White was simply a pawn up with a better position. 12...♘xe5? should be replaced with the far more satisfactory 12...♗xe5. For example, 13 ♗h6 ♗g7 14 ♗xg7 ♔xg7 and the black queen will arrive at f6 to ensure equality.

10...e5 11 dxe5 ♕xd1 12 ♗xd1 ♘c4

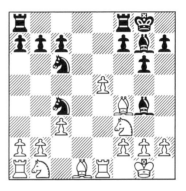

13 ♘fd2

13 ♘bd2! seems to cause Black a few more problems. The game Klovan-Dautov, USSR 1986, continued 13...♘xb2 14 ♗c2 ♖ad8 15 ♖ab1 ♘d3 16 ♗xd3 ♖xd3 17 ♖xb7 ♘d8 18 ♖xc7 ♘e6 19 ♖c4 ♘xf4 20 ♖xf4 ♗e6 21 ♖a4 ♖xc3. In his notes to the game in *Informator 42*, Dautov assesses this position as being equal, and after Klovan's 22 ♘d4 the game finally ended in a draw. Dautov fails to suggest the obvious 22 ♖xa7. Black certainly has some compensation in the shape of the bishop pair, but is it really worth two pawns?

13...♘4xe5 14 ♗xg4 ♘d3!

A nice finesse. 14...♘xg4 15 ♗xc7 is

simply a pawn.

15 ♖e3

After 15 ♖e4? f5! 16 ♖c4 fxg4, the threats against f4 and b2 give Black the advantage, but after the game move an equal endgame is reached.

15...♘xf4 16 ♘a3 ♘d5 17 ♖ee1 ♘e5 18 ♗e2 ♘f4 19 ♘dc4 ♘ed3 20 g3 ♘xe2+ 21 ♖xe2 a6 22 ♖d1 ♘c5 23 ♘e3 ♖fe8 24 ♘ac4 b5 25 ♘a5 ♖ad8 26 ♖xd8 ♖xd8 27 ♔g2 ♔f8 28 ♘c2

This is the beginning of a strange two knight dance by White.

28...♖d6 29 ♘b4 ♘a4 30 ♘bc6 ♗f6 31 ♘b8 ♔g7 32 ♘ac6

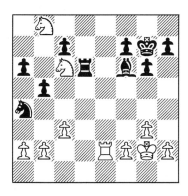

32...♘c5 33 ♖c2 ♘d3 34 ♔f1 ♘e5 35 ♘xe5 ♗xe5 36 ♖e2 ♗f6 37 ♔e1 c5 38 ♖d2 ♖e6+ 39 ♖e2 ♖d6

Repetition is the safest course for Black. After 39...♖xe2+ 40 ♔xe2 a5 41 a4 bxa4 42 ♔d3 White's active king gives him all the winning chances.

40 ♖d2 ♖e6+ 41 ♖e2 ♖d6 ½-½

Game 53
Vitolinsh-Dautov
Daugavpils 1989

1 e4 d5 2 exd5 ♘f6 3 d4 ♘xd5 4

♘f3 ♗g4 5 h3 ♗h5 6 g4!?

Lunging forward on the kingside. 6 c4 would transpose to Chapter 6 after 6...♘b6 or 6...♘f6.

6...♗g6 7 ♘e5

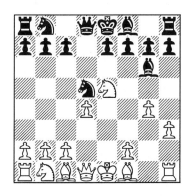

7...♘d7

The alternative 7...♘c6 led to a plus for White after 8 ♘xg6 hxg6 9 ♗g2 ♕d6 10 0-0 ♘f4 11 ♗xf4 ♕xf4 12 ♘c3 0-0-0 13 ♘e2 ♕d6 14 c3 f5 15 ♘g3 e5 16 gxf5 exd4 in Aseev-Gipslis, Brno 1991. Here Aseev suggests 17 ♕g4 as the best continuation for White.

8 ♘xg6 hxg6 9 ♗g2 e6!?

A tricky move-order. Other encounters have continued 9...c6 10 c4 and now:

a) 10...♘5b6 11 ♕e2 ♘f6 (11...e6! may be the strongest move, transposing to the main game and not allowing g4-g5 ideas) 12 ♗e3 (Razuvaev likes 12 g5!? ♘h5 13 d5, opening the game up for the two bishops) 12...e6 13 ♘c3 ♗e7 (13...♗b4!) 14 0-0-0 and White had an edge in Razuvaev-Gipslis, USSR 1973.

b) 10...♘5f6 11 ♕e2 ♕a5+ 12 ♘c3 0-0-0 13 d5! cxd5 14 cxd5 ♘b6 15 ♗d2 ♕a6 16 ♕xa6 bxa6 17 ♖c1 ♔b7 18

♗e3 with a huge attack, Kotronias-Efthimiou, Ano Liosia Open 1995.

10 c4 ♘5b6 11 ♕e2

Why not 11 ♗xb7 here? Well, Dautov presumably intended 11...♘xc4 12 ♗xa8 ♕xa8 13 f3 c5, when the weaknesses around the white king offer Black some play for the sacrificed exchange.

11...c6 12 ♘c3 ♗b4 13 0-0 0-0 14 c5 ♘d5 15 ♘e4 ♗a5!

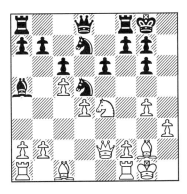

This bishop has a good future on the h2-b8 diagonal, where it will eye the draughty squares around the white king. Despite his space disadvantage, Black stands reasonably well.

16 f4 ♗c7 17 ♗d2 ♘7f6 18 ♖ad1 ♘xe4 19 ♕xe4 ♕d7 20 ♕f3 b6 21 f5 gxf5 22 gxf5 ♖ae8 23 b4 ♗b8 24 ♖f2 ♕c7 25 ♗f1 exf5 26 ♕xf5 ♖e3! 27 ♗xe3 ♘xe3 28 ♕f3 ♘xd1 29 ♕xd1 ♕g3+ 30 ♗g2 ♖e8 31 ♔f1

I would imagine that the players were drifting into time-trouble around this stage, as they are both guilty of some inaccurate moves before time control is reached.

31...♕c3

31...♖e6, protecting c6, looks stronger.

32 ♗xc6 ♖e6 33 ♗d5 ♖h6? 34 ♗g2?

34 ♕g4!, threatening ♕c8+, forces Black into a miserable endgame with 34...♕xh3+ 35 ♕xh3 ♖xh3 36 ♖xf7, when White's c- and d-pawns should prevail.

34...♕e3 35 ♖f3 ♕g5 36 d5 ♖g6

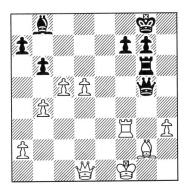

37 ♕e2??

37 ♖f2! was necessary.

37...♗g3??

After 37...♕c1+ 38 ♔f2 ♗h2! Black gets 'round the back', and the threat of ♕g1 mate forces White to give up at least a piece.

38 ♕e3 ♗f4 39 ♕xf4 ♕xg2+ 40 ♔e1 ♕h1+ 41 ♔e2 ½-½

Probably a fair result. After 41...♖g2+ 42 ♖f2 ♖xf2+ 43 ♔xf2 ♕xd5 44 ♕b8+ ♔h7 45 ♕xa7 ♕d4+ 46 ♔f3 ♕c3+ 47 ♔g2 ♕d2+ White cannot cross fourth rank with his king without allowing the b- and c-pawns to fall.

> *Game 54*
> **Kindermann-Schmitzer**
> *Germany 1995*

1 e4 d5 2 exd5 ♘f6 3 d4 ♘xd5 4

♘f3 ♗g4 5 ♗e2 e6 6 0-0 ♗e7

The most flexible choice. 6...♘d7 was treated roughly in Godena-Smagin, Vienna 1991, which continued 7 c4 ♘5b6 (perhaps 7...♘f6 is safer) 8 ♘c3 ♗e7 9 c5! ♘c8 (not a nice retreat but 9...♘d5 10 ♘xd5 exd5 11 ♕b3 attacks b7 and d5) 10 ♗f4 0-0 11 h3 ♗h5 12 ♕b3 b6 13 ♘b5 c6 14 ♗c7 ♕e8 15 ♘d6 ♘xd6 16 cxd6 with a horrible position for Black.

7 ♘e5!

One useful point of delaying c2-c4, is that the black knight on d5 blocks the attack on White's d4-pawn, allowing White's queen to move from d1.

7...♗xe2 8 ♕xe2 0-0

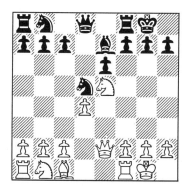

9 c4

A recent game Leko-Kamsky, Groningen 1995, saw White build up a promising position after 9 ♖d1 ♘d7 10 c4 ♘5f6 11 ♗f4 c6 12 ♘c3 ♖e8 13 ♖d3 ♘f8 14 ♖ad1 ♕a5 15 a3 ♘g6 16 ♗g3 ♖ac8. Now Leko recommends 17 h4! ♖ed8 18 h5 ♘xe5 19 dxe5 ♘e8 20 ♘e4 with a clear plus for White.

9...♘b4?!

This turns out to be the root of all Black's future problems. The usual 9...♘f6 and 9...♘b6 are both stronger.

10 ♖d1 ♘8c6 11 ♘f3!

Exchanging knights would have relieved Black's cramped pieces. Now the knight on b4 is embarassed.

11...a5 12 ♘c3 ♖e8 13 ♗e3 ♗f8 14 a3 ♘a6 15 ♕c2 h6 16 d5 exd5 17 ♘xd5 ♗c5 18 ♗f4 ♕c8 19 ♖e1 ♕g4

With Black's pieces cluttering up the queenside, White has a clear plus. Black was obviously eager to connect the rooks, but this move allows White to win a pawn, which is enough to decide the game.

20 ♗xh6! ♘d4

As 20...gxh6 runs into 21 ♘f6+.

21 ♘xd4 ♗xd4 22 ♗e3 c6 23 ♗xd4 cxd5 24 ♕c3 dxc4 25 h3 ♕f4 26 ♗xg7 ♘c5 27 ♗e5 ♕h4 28 ♗g3 ♕h7 29 ♕xc4 ♘d3 30 ♖xe8+ ♖xe8

31 ♖d1! ♘xb2 32 ♕b5 ♘xd1 33 ♕xe8+ ♔g7 34 ♗e5+ ♔g6 35 ♕d8 ♕h5 36 ♕f6+ 1-0.

It is mate next move.

Summary

If Black cannot find an improvement on the critical Campora-Maliutin encounter (Game 48), then there is always the rock-solid 7...c6 to fall back on. 5 ♗c4 does not present Black with too many problems, as there is more than one way to attack White's centre. 4...♗g4 still requires some more top-level clashes before a definite assessment can be made.

1 e4 d5 2 exd5 ♘f6 3 d4 ♘xd5 4 ♘f3

4...g6
      4...♗g4 *(D)*
            5 h3 - *game 53*
            5 ♗e2 - *game 54*
5 ♗e2
      5 ♗c4 ♗g7 6 0-0 *(D)*
            6...♘b6 - *game 51*
            6...0-0 - *game 52*
5...♗g7 6 0-0 0-0 7 ♖e1 *(D)*
      7 h3 - *game 50*
7...c5 - *game 48*
7...c6 - *game 49*

4...♗g4

6 0-0

7 ♖e1

CHAPTER EIGHT

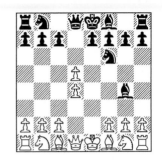

2...♘f6: 3 d4 ♗g4!?

1 e4 d5 2 exd5 ♘f6 3 d4 ♗g4!?

In the late 1980s, the Belgian masters Jadoul and Vandevoort introduced the tricky line 1 e4 d5 2 exd5 ♘f6 3 d4 ♗g4!? with reasonable success. Perhaps due to the lack of a high profile victory, this variation never received the same attention as the Icelandic Gambit and remained in obscurity until 1992, when Portuguese IMs Galego and Damaso notched up some particularly quick wins with it. Since then its popularity has steadily increased and it has even received an outing from the English GM Julian Hodgson, who has never been afraid to experiment.

3...♗g4 cannot be taken lightly. Practical results have been quite good for Black and it certainly catches players off guard. White has three main replies. In order of importance they are 4 f3, 4 ♗e2 and 4 ♘f3. 4 ♗b5+ has no real independent value, as after 4...♘bd7 White has nothing better than 5 f3 ♗f5, transposing to 4 f3 ♗f5 5 ♗b5+ ♘bd7.

With 4 f3 White signals the intention of keeping the extra pawn. After 4...♗f5 5 ♗b5+ ♘bd7 6 c4 (Games 55-56), play becomes very sharp, with

variations similar to the Icelandic Gambit. 5 c4 is also possible, although Black seems to have all the fun (Game 57).

The fact that White has found nothing concrete with 4 f3 has led to a few games with the sensible 4 ♗e2, the choice of John Nunn and Peter Leko when facing 3...♗g4. With 4 ♗e2 (Games 58-59) White gives up all claims for a large advantage, but is comforted by the fact that one is unlikely to be checkmated in less than 25 moves, not an infrequent occurrence with 4 f3.

4 ♘f3 ♕xd5 (Game 60) has scored particularly well for Black. In contrast to 2...♕xd5 the black queen has some extra possibilities when attacked. Depending on circumstances, h5, f5 and d7 can all be useful retreat squares.

Game 55
Lanka-Hauchard
Torcy 1991

---

1 e4 d5 2 exd5 ♘f6 3 d4 ♗g4 4 f3 ♗f5 5 ♗b5+

5 c4 will be discussed in Game 57. We could also reach this position via the move order 4 ♗b5+ ♘bd7 5 f3

♗f5. Note that in this line 4...c6 can be answered simply with 5 dxc6, as 5...♗xd1 6 c7+ wins for White.

5...♘bd7 6 c4 a6

6...e6 is considered in the next game.

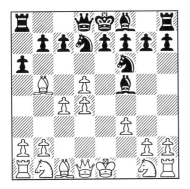

7 ♗xd7+

After 7 ♗a4 Black should not hesitate to lash out with 7...b5! 8 cxb5 ♘b6 (or 7...♘xd5!?) 9 bxa6+ (after 9 ♗b3 axb5, the d5-pawn will be rounded up) 9...♘xa4 10 ♕xa4+ ♗d7 and now on 11 ♕a5?! Black simply replies 11...♕c8! 12 ♘e2 ♖xa6 with fantastic compensation for the material. 11 ♕b3 is more sensible, but 11...♖xa6 still leaves Black with plenty of play.

7...♕xd7 8 ♘e2 e6!

It is imperative that Black blasts open the centre as quickly as possible, in order to exploit his lead in development.

9 dxe6 ♕xe6 10 b3! 0-0-0 11 0-0 ♗c5! 12 ♔h1!

12 ♘bc3 allows 12...♕e5!, and Black will simply capture the d-pawn with an equal position. Still, Black has another neat idea to restore material balance.

12...♗xd4! 13 ♘xd4 ♕d7 14 ♗b2

14 ♗e3 c5 15 ♘xf5 fails to 15...♕xd1 16 ♖xd1 ♖xd1+ 17 ♗g1 ♖e8 and the threat of ...♖ee1 is decisive.

14...c5 15 b4! cxd4 16 b5!

16...axb5?!

In this position, where the players have castled on opposite wings, the initiative becomes much more significant than a lowly pawn. 16...♖he8 seems to be the way forward for Black, when after 17 bxa6 bxa6 18 ♘d2 d3 19 ♖b1 ♖e2 we have a finely balanced position. Black's pieces are more actively posted, while he also holds a menacing passed pawn on d3. On the other hand, his king is by far the more exposed. I am afraid that I shall have to sit on the fence here with a chunky 'unclear' assessment.

17 ♘a3 bxc4 18 ♘xc4 ♔b8 19 ♗a3!

Excellent play by Lanka. The dark squares on the queenside are beginning to look extremely vulnerable.

19...♕d5 20 ♖c1 ♖he8 21 ♕d2 ♖e6 22 ♘a5!

The threats are coming thick and fast. The first is 23 ♖c5, which would win a piece.

22...♕b5 23 ♗c5!

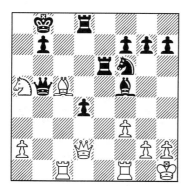

This time the idea is ♕f4+, again winning a piece.

23...♔a8 24 a4 ♕a6 25 ♘b3! ♗d3 26 ♖g1 ♖e2 27 ♕b4 ♘h5

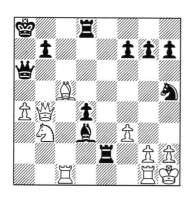

Recognising that he is totally busted, Black plays for tricks. If allowed ...♘g3+ and ...♕h6 mate would follow.

28 ♗b6! ♖de8 29 ♘c5 ♖8e5 30 ♖gd1

Again preventing ...♘g3+. Now the black queen is trapped, while 30...♖xc5 31 ♕xc5 and a major piece will land on c8 so...

1-0

A significant game. In the end it was quite comfortable for the Latvian Grandmaster, but from a theoretical standpoint Black has no reason to complain.

Game 56
Votava-Ribeiro
Erevan Olympiad 1996

1 e4 d5 2 exd5 ♘f6 3 d4 ♗g4 4 ♗b5+ ♘bd7 5 f3 ♗f5 6 c4 e6 7 dxe6 ♗xe6 8 ♘c3 ♗b4 9 d5 ♗f5 10 ♘ge2 0-0 11 ♗xd7!

An important move. After 11 0-0 ♘e5! the bishop on b5 becomes rather stuck out on a limb, and this is the last chance to off-load it.

11...♘xd7

Following 11...♕xd7 12 0-0 c6, White has the irritating 13 ♗g5.

12 0-0 ♘e5 13 ♔h1!?

Jettisoning the c-pawn, although it is not clear whether Black has enough play after the materialistic 13 b3. In the only other example from this position White also gave back the c-pawn after 13 ♘g3 ♗d7 14 ♔h1 ♘xc4 15 ♕d4 b5 16 ♘ce4 with a tiny edge for White in Van der Wiel-An.Fernandes, Linares Zonal 1995.

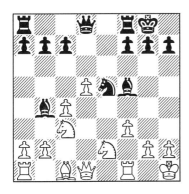

13...♕h4

This meets with a powerful refutation. Black is only slightly worse after 13...♘xc4 14 ♕d4 ♗xc3 15 bxc3 b5 16 ♘g3 ♗d7 (or 16...♗g6!?) 17 ♗f4.

14 ♘g3 ♗d3 15 ♘ce4 ♕d8

White was threatening ♗g5, trapping the black queen. Superficially this position looks perfectly okay for Black, whose double attack on f1 and c4 seems to regain the sacrificed pawn. However, there is a nasty surprise.

16 f4! ♗xf1 17 fxe5 ♗xc4 18 ♘f5!

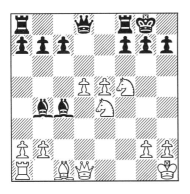

...and suddenly Black is totally lost. The threat of ♕g4 is unstoppable.

18...♗xd5

Other losing lines include:
a) 18...♔h8 19 ♕g4 ♖g8 20 ♘g5

♗xd5 21 e6! ♗xe6 22 ♕h5 h6 23 ♘xh6!

b) 18...g6 19 ♘f6+ ♔h8 20 ♕g4 and 21 ♕h4.

19 ♕g4 g6 20 ♘f6+ ♔h8 21 ♕h4 h5 22 ♕g5 1-0

There's no defence to ♕h6 mate.

Game 57
Burovic-Monange
Torcy 1991

1 e4 d5 2 exd5 ♘f6 3 d4 ♗g4 4 f3 ♗f5 5 c4

This seemingly natural way to hold onto the pawn allows Black a surprisingly menacing second gambit.

5...e6 6 dxe6 ♘c6!

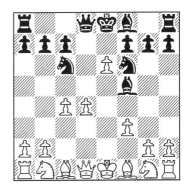

The whole point. Black does not waste time on trivial recaptures, but instead develops at lightning speed. This line can be considered as a 'beefed up' Icelandic Gambit. Needless to say, White has to proceed with the utmost care, and even this may not be enough to survive.

7 ♘e2

With this move White offers back some material with the intention of completing his development and consolidating. There are two other critical choices:

a) 7 d5 ♘b4 8 ♘a3!?

b) 7 exf7+?! (a rather gluttonous idea that unsurprisingly falls into a devastating attack) 7...♔xf7 8 ♗e3 ♗b4+ and now:

b1) 9 ♘c3 ♖e8 10 ♔f2 ♖xe3! 11 ♔xe3 ♘xd4 12 ♕xd4 ♕e7+ and White must off-load the queen with 13 ♔d2 ♖d8. 13 ♔f2 ♗c5 is even worse, while 13 ♔f4 allows mate after 13...♘h5+ 14 ♔xf5 ♕e6+ 15 ♔g5 ♗e7+ 16 ♔xh5 ♕g6 (Burgess).

b2) 9 ♔f2 ♖e8 10 ♘e2 ♖xe3! 11 ♔xe3 ♕e7+ 12 ♔f2 ♖e8 13 ♕c1 ♘xd4! 14 ♘xd4 ♗e1+ 15 ♔g1 ♕c5 16 ♕d1 ♗c2! 0-1 Dimitrov-Rivera, Lalin 1994.

7...♘b4 8 ♘g3 ♘c2+ 9 ♔f2 ♗g6 10 ♗e3

10...♗c5!?

Black continues to play in the most adventurous way. Objectively, it may be best to cash in one's chips with the materialistic 10...♘xa1. After all, a rook is a rook. After 11 ♗d3 ♗xd3 12 ♕xd3 fxe6 13 ♘c3 ♗d6 14 ♖xa1 0-0 White has a pawn for the exchange, which is probably not sufficient. 12

exf7+, grabbing a second pawn, is possibly stronger.

11 ♘a3 ♘xe3 12 ♔xe3 ♘g4+! 13 fxg4 ♕g5+

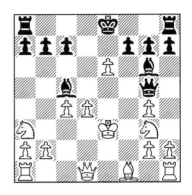

14 ♔f3?

14 ♔e2 was the only move. After 14...♕xg4+ 15 ♔e1 ♕xe6+ 16 ♗e2 Black still has to justify the piece sacrifice.

14...fxe6! 15 ♗d3 0-0+ 16 ♘f5

16 ♔e2 ♗xd4 17 ♘c2 ♕e5+ 18 ♗e4 ♗f2 wins for Black.

16...exf5 17 dxc5 fxg4+ 18 ♔g3 h5 19 h3

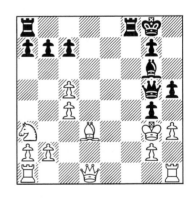

19...h4+ 20 ♔h2 g3+ 21 ♔g1 ♕e3 mate

A pretty finish to a totally wild game. Needless to say, not many

White players are willing to be exposed to such a ferocious attack, so I don't predict a bright future for 5 c4.

Game 58
Atlas-Hodgson
Germany 1996

---

1 e4 d5 2 exd5 ♘f6 3 d4 ♗g4 4 ♗e2 ♗xe2 5 ♕xe2

The strongest continuation. 5 ♘xe2 seems a little too passive. After 5...♕xd5 6 0-0 ♘c6!? 7 ♘bc3 ♕h5 8 ♗e3 0-0-0 9 ♕d3 ♘g4 10 h3 ♘xe3 11 fxe3?! e5 12 ♕e4 f6 13 d5 ♘b4 14 ♘g3 ♕g6 15 ♘f5 ♕f7 Black was clearly better in De Vuyst-Joseph, Correspondence 1989, although White's play left a lot to be desired.

5...♕xd5 6 ♘f3 ♘c6!?

This may be a bit too provocative. The safer 6...e6 will be examined in Game 59.

7 c4 ♕f5 8 0-0 e6

9 ♗e3

9 d5! looks very effective here, as after 9...♘b4 10 a3! ♘c2 11 ♖a2, b2-b4 is difficult to meet.

9...♗d6 10 ♘c3 0-0 11 ♖ad1 ♖fe8

Intending 12...e5.

12 ♕d3

Here 12 ♖fe1!? is stronger with the following alternatives:

a) 12...e5 13 d5 e4? 14 ♘h4 ♕e5 15 g3 ♘b4 16 ♗d4 and the critical e4-pawn drops.

b) 12...♖ad8 is better, although White still retains a slight pull.

12...♕h5?!

12...♕xd3 13 ♖xd3 e5 equalises after 14 dxe5 ♘xe5 15 ♘xe5 ♗xe5 or 14 d5 ♘a5 15 c5 e4. Now White obtains a very pleasant endgame.

13 ♘e4 ♘xe4 14 ♕xe4 f5 15 ♕h4! ♕xh4 16 ♘xh4

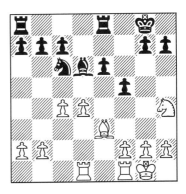

16...f4 17 ♗c1 g5 18 ♘f3 h6 19 ♖fe1 ♖ad8 20 g4! ♔f7

Or 20...e5 21 d5! ♘b8 22 ♘d2 and the knight has a dominating post on e4.

21 ♔g2 ♗b4 22 ♖e4 ♗e7 23 ♗d2! ♗f6 24 ♗c3 a6 25 h4 b5 26 b3 b4 27 ♗b2 ♖d6 28 hxg5 hxg5 29 ♖h1 ♖g8?

A blunder in a difficult position. 29...♔g6 hangs on.

30 ♖h7+ ♖g7 31 ♖xg7+ ♔xg7 32 c5 ♖d8 33 ♖xe6 ♘e7 34 ♖xa6 ♘d5 35 a3 ♖e8 36 ♘e5

White has played excellently to

build up a totally winning position, but now a series of second-best moves spoil things. 36 ♔f1!, preventing ...♖e2, would have been the end for Black.

36...bxa3 37 ♖xa3?

Another time-trouble error. 37 ♗xa3 ♖b8 38 b4 ♗xe5 39 dxe5 ♘xb4 40 ♗xb4 ♖xb4 41 ♖a7 is sufficient for victory.

37...♗xe5 38 dxe5 ♖b8! 39 ♔f3 ♖b4 40 e6+ ♔f8 41 ♗e5 ♔e7 42 ♖a6 ♖xb3+ 43 ♔e4 ♘b4 44 ♖a7 ♔xe6 45 ♖xc7 ♖b1 46 ♗d6?

46 ♗d4 was the last chance to play for the win.

46...♘d5! 47 ♖g7 ♘f6+ 48 ♔d4 ♖d1+ 49 ♔c4 ♖c1+ 50 ♔b5 ♘e4 51 ♔c6 ♘xd6 52 ♖g6+ ♔e5 53 ♖xd6 ♔e4 54 ♖d5 ♔f3 55 ♔d6 ♔xf2 56 ♖xg5 ♔g3 57 c6 f3 58 c7 f2 59 ♖f5 ♖d1+ 60 ♔e6 ♖c1 61 ♔d6 ♖d1+ 62 ♔e6 ♖c1 63 ♔d6 ½-½

After 63 ♔d7 ♖d1+ 64 ♔c8 f1♕ 65 ♖xf1 ♖xf1 66 g5 ♔h4 67 g6 ♖g1 68 ♔d7 ♖d1+ 69 ♔e6 ♖e1+ 70 ♔d7 ♖d1+ 71 ♔c8 ♖g1 72 ♔b7 ♖b1+ White cannot escape the checks without allowing the black rook to the back rank.

Game 59
Leko-Damaso
Erevan Olympiad 1996

1 e4 d5 2 exd5 ♘f6 3 d4 ♗g4 4 ♗e2 ♗xe2 5 ♕xe2 ♕xd5 6 ♘f3 e6 7 c4 ♕f5 8 0-0 ♗e7 9 ♘c3 0-0 10 d5

Already one can see the advantage of delaying ...♘c6 in this line: White's d4-d5 does not come with a gain of tempo.

11...♗c5 11 dxe6

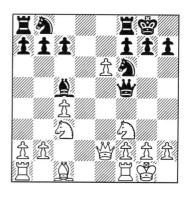

11...♘c6!

A good pawn sacrifice. After 11...♕xe6 12 ♕xe6 fxe6 13 ♖e1 Black will suffer in the endgame due to the chronic weakness on e6.

12 ♗e3 ♖ae8 13 ♗xc5

The safe option, although after this move White cannot claim to have any advantage whatsoever. Nevertheless following 13 exf7+ ♖xf7 Black's active pieces and the threat of ...♘g4 gives White a few headaches.

13...♕xc5 14 exf7+ ♖xf7 15 ♕c2 ♕xc4

Black has regained the pawn with a completely level position.

16 ♖fe1 ♖fe7 17 ♖xe7 ♖xe7 18 ♖d1 ♘e4 19 ♘d2 ♘xd2 20 ♕xd2 ♘d4 21 h3 c5 22 ♕g5 ♖e8 23 ♕h5 ♖e6 24 ♔h2 b6 25 ♕g4 ♖e8 26 f3 h6 27 ♕d7 ♕f7 28 ♕xf7+ ♔xf7 29 ♔g3

29...♖d8?!

If Black was after a draw, then 29...♘e2+ is the simplest method. Then both 30 ♘xe2 ♖xe2 31 ♖d7+ ♔f6 32 ♖xa7 ♖xb2 and 30 ♔f2 ♘xc3 31 bxc3 ♖e7 offer White no chances.
30 ♔f2 ♘c6 31 ♖xd8 ♘xd8 32 ♔e3 ♘c6 33 ♔e4 ♔e6 34 f4 ♘d4 35 g4 ♔d6 36 f5 b5 37 h4 a5? 38 a4!

38...bxa4

After 38...b4 39 ♘b5+ ♘xb5 40 axb5 White has passed pawns on both sides, which prove to be decisive, e.g.

40...a4 41 ♔d3 ♔d5 42 b6 c4+ 43 ♔c2 ♔c6 44 g5 hxg5 45 hxg5 ♔xb6 46 f6 gxf6 47 gxf6 and the pawn promotes. Hence Black is forced to compromise his structure, giving White excellent winning chances.
39 ♘xa4 ♘b3 40 ♘b6 ♘d2+ 41 ♔f4 ♔e7 42 g5 hxg5+ 43 hxg5 ♔f7 44 ♘d7 c4 45 ♘e5+ ♔f8 46 ♔e3 c3 47 bxc3 ♘f1+ 48 ♔f4 a4 49 ♘c4 ♔e7 50 ♔e5 ♘g3 51 ♘a3 ♘e2 52 c4 ♘g1 53 c5 ♘f3+ 54 ♔f4 ♘d4 55 ♔e4 ♘e2 56 ♔e5 ♘g1 57 f6+ gxf6+ 58 gxf6+ ♔e8 59 c6 ♘f3+ 60 ♔d6 1-0

60...♘g5 61 c7 ♘f7+ 62 ♔e6 ♘g5+ 63 ♔f5 is terminal. Good technique from Leko, but another theoretical success for 3...♗g4.

Game 60
Mortensen-Damaso
Debrecen 1992

---

1 e4 d5 2 exd5 ♘f6 3 d4

Let us take a brief look at White's alternatives here:

a) 3 ♘f3!? is a move that we may start to see more of in the future, especially if no firm antidote is found against 3 d4 ♗g4!? The point is that Black seems to have nothing better than to return to the main lines with either 3...♕xd5 or 3...♘xd5, although in the process this has ruled out some early c2-c4 options for White. In contrast, 3...♗g4 just looks as though it should not work. After 4 ♗b5+ ♘bd7 5 c4 White has not been forced to compromise the kingside pawn structure. The continuations 5...a6 6 ♗xd7+ ♕xd7 7 d4 and 5...a6 6 ♗a4 both look good for White, while 5 h3 ♗xf3 6 ♕xf3 a6 7 ♗a4 b5 8 ♗b3 ♘b6 9 ♘c3 b4 10 ♘e4 is also strong, as 10...♘fxd5 fails to 11 ♘g5 f6 12 ♘e6, 13 ♗xd5 and 14 ♕xd5!

b) 3 ♘c3 transposes to a harmless line of the Alekhine Defence (1 e4 ♘f6 2 ♘c3 d5 3 exd5). Following 3...♘xd5 4 ♗c4 ♘b6 5 ♗b3 ♘c6 6 ♘f3 ♗f5! 7 d4 e6 Black can look to the future with confidence. Lein-Alburt, New York 1980, continued 8 ♗f4?! ♗d6 9 ♕d2 0-0 10 ♗g3 ♗g4 11 0-0-0 ♘a5! and Black was already better. 8 0-0 is stronger, but in any case Black has no worries.

3...♗g4 4 ♘f3 ♕xd5 5 ♘c3 ♕f5

The substantial advantage Black has over the normal 2...♕xd5 lines, is that the queen now has many more available options. 5...♕h5 also cannot be discounted, when after 6 ♗e2 ♘c6 7 h3 0-0-0 8 0-0 play becomes razor sharp with 8...♘xd4! 9 ♘xd4 ♗xe2 and now:

a) 10 ♘cxe2 e5 11 ♗e3 ♗c5 12 c3 exd4 13 ♘xd4 ♕g6 was equal in Tin-ture-Brebion, Correspondence 1992.

b) 10 ♕xe2!? ♖xd4 11 ♕e3 (11 ♕xh5 ♘xh5 12 ♘b5 looks stronger) 11...e5 12 ♘b5 ♖d1 13 g4? (13 ♘xa7+ ♔b8 14 ♘b5 ♖xf1+ 15 ♔xf1 ♗c5! is better for Black, as 16 ♕xc5 allows mate on d1, but this is suicide) 13...♘xg4! 14 hxg4 ♕xg4+ 15 ♕g3 ♖xf1+ 16 ♔xf1 ♕d1+ and White resigned on account of 17 ♔g2 ♕d5+ Keitlinghaus-Zvara, Ceske Budejovice Open 1995.

6 ♗e2 ♘c6 7 ♗e3?!

After the preferred 7 d5 Black does not play 7...0-0-0?, as in Hjartarson-Galego, Oviedo (rapidplay) 1992, because 8 ♗d3 simply wins a piece. Instead 7...♘b4 8 ♘d4 ♗xe2 9 ♕xe2 ♕d7 is the best bet. Now White cannot hold on to the d5-pawn, although after 10 0-0 ♘bxd5 11 ♘xd5 ♘xd5 12 ♖d1, he does have some play for it.

7...0-0-0 8 0-0 e5 9 d5 ♘b4

Attacking pawns on c2 and d5. Black is already doing very well.

10 h3 ♗xf3 11 ♗xf3 ♔b8 12 g4 ♕g6 13 ♕e2 h5 14 g5 ♘xc2 15 ♘b5 ♘d4!

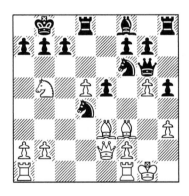

16 ♘xd4 exd4 17 ♗xd4 ♕xg5+ 18 ♗g2 ♘xd5 19 ♕f3 c6 20 ♖fe1 ♗d6 21 ♖e4 ♗c7 22 b4 f5! 23 ♖e5 ♘f4 0-1

A fine game by Damaso.

Summary

Despite a White victory in the critical Lanka-Hauchard encounter (Game 55), Black has definite improvements which very much cloud the issue. 4 ♗e2 may just about be enough for a minute edge, while 4 ♘f3 ♕xd5 seems absolutely fine for the second player.

1 e4 d5 2 exd5 ♘f6 3 d4 ♗g4

4 f3 *(D)*
    4 ♗b5+ ♘bd7 5 f3 ♗f5 - see 4 f3 ♗f5 5 ♗b5+ ♘bd7 below
    4 ♗e2 ♗xe2 5 ♕xe2 ♕xd5 6 ♘f3 *(D)*
        6...♘c6 - *game 58*
        6...e6 - *game 59*
    4 ♘f3 - *game 60*
4...♗f5 5 ♗b5+
    5 c4 - *game 57*
5...♘bd7 6 c4 *(D)*
    6...a6 - *game 55*
    6...e6 - *game 56*

    4 f3   *6 ♘f3*   *6 c4*

CHAPTER NINE

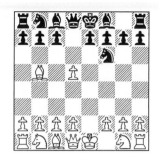

2...♘f6: 3 ♗b5+

1 e4 d5 2 exd5 ♘f6 3 ♗b5+

3 ♗b5+ is a risky move which disrupts Black's basic plan of regaining the d5-pawn. Following 3...♗d7 and the less common 3...♘bd7, Black often has to be prepared to give up attempts to win back the material. As far as White is concerned, hanging on to the d5-pawn usually entails some sort of cost, either structurally or in development, and it is here that Black can seek compensation.

Notwithstanding the above, after 3...♗d7 a popular try is 4 ♗e2 (Games 61 and 62), simply returning the pawn at the first possible moment. The idea is that following 4...♘xd5 5 d4, the bishop would prefer to stand on c8 rather than d7, where it looks totally misplaced. Black usually addresses this problem immediately with 5...♗f5, followed by simple development with ...e7-e6, ...♗e7 and ...0-0.

4 ♗c4 is the most principled choice, after which Black has to decide between 4...♗g4 (Games 63-67) and Bronstein's favourite 4...b5!? (Game 68). Play is generally quite complex and many assessments hang in the balance.

3 ♗b5+ ♘bd7!? (Game 69) is a bla-

tant pawn sacrifice by Black which leads to very interesting positions. Surprisingly 3...♘bd7 remains rare at tournament level, although there is no clear refutation to it.

> ### Game 61
> ### Kupreichik-Gipslis
> *Alborg 1993*

1 e4 d5 2 exd5 ♘f6 3 ♗b5+ ♗d7 4 ♗e2

The solid option. 4 ♗c4 will be discussed later.

4...♘xd5 5 d4 ♗f5 6 ♘f3 e6 7 0-0 ♗e7 8 c4!?

This move, attacking the knight immediately, has the advantage of not wasting a move with a2-a3, but of course it does allow the black knight to occupy the b4-square. For 8 a3 see the next game.

8...♘b4 9 ♘a3

A necessity, as 9 ♘c3 gives Black the option of at least a draw with 9...♘c2 10 ♖b1 ♘b4.

9...0-0 10 ♗f4

see following diagram

10...♘8c6

Perhaps Black should consider

10...a6 or 10...c6 here to prevent ♘b5.

11 ♘b5! ♖c8 12 a3 a6 13 d5!

Kupreichik, a dangerous tactician, thrives on these complications. 13 axb4? axb5 14 cxb5 ♘xb4 would have been fine for Black, who has a ready-made outpost for the knight on d5.

13...axb5

13...exd5? uncovers the point of 13 d5: 14 ♘bd4! leaves Black with two pieces hanging.

14 dxc6 ♘d3!

This incursion is Black's best try. The timid 14...♘xc6 15 cxb5 is clearly better for White, as the black knight is short of good squares, e.g. 15...♘a7 16 ♕a4!, followed by ♖fd1.

15 cxb7 ♖b8 16 ♗xd3 ♗xd3

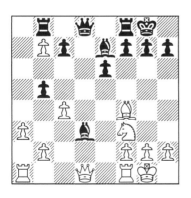

17 ♘e5!

The only way to play for an advantage. Black has no problems after 17 ♗xc7 ♕xc7 18 ♕xd3 bxc4 19 ♖ac1 ♕xb7 20 ♕xc4 ♕xb2.

17...♗xf1 18 ♕xf1! ♕e8!?

18...♖xb7 is similar to the game after 19 ♘c6 ♕d7 20 cxb5, although in this case White retains the knight. This would probably be to his advantage as it supports the queenside pawns well from the c6-post.

19 cxb5 ♗d6 20 a4 ♖xb7 21 ♕c4 ♗xe5 22 ♗xe5 ♕d7 23 h3

Despite having only one pawn for the exchange, White's threatening queenside pawns plus the chronic weakness on c7 add up to a significant advantage.

23...f6 24 ♗f4 ♔h8 25 ♖c1 e5 26 ♗e3 ♖d8 27 b4 h6 28 ♔h2 f5

This lunge forward on the kingside seems to be Black's best bet to confuse matters. The endgame arising after 28...♕d5 29 ♕xd5 ♖xd5 30 ♖c6 brings him no relief. White may simply play a timely b5-b6!, leaving two powerful passed pawns for Black to contend with.

29 ♖c2 ♕d5 30 ♕c3!? ♖a8 31 ♖d2

♛e6 32 ♕c2 f4 33 ♗c5 e4 34 ♖d4

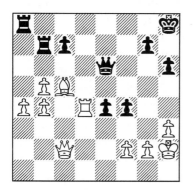

A critical moment. Black would like to carry on his kingside offensive with the natural looking 34...e3, but Kupreichik gives a fantastic refutation to this: White can play 35 ♖e4! exf2 36 ♖xe6 f1♕ 37 ♖xh6+! gxh6 38 ♗d4+ and Black is mated after 38...♚g8 39 ♕g6+ ♚f8 40 ♗c5.

34...♖e8 35 ♕e2!

White has tamed Black's ambitions on the kingside and is now ready to advance with 36 a5. Gipslis decided to throw caution to the wind in a desperate last assault.

35...f3!? 36 gxf3 ♕e5+ 37 ♚h1 ♕h5 38 ♖xe4 ♕xh3+ 39 ♚g1 ♖xe4 40 fxe4 ♖b8 41 a5?!

This complicates matters. 41 e5! would have been more accurate.

41...♖xb5! 42 e5

As 42 ♕xb5 allows a perpetual check starting with 42...♕g4+.

42...♕e6 43 f4 ♖b8 44 a6 c6 45 a7 ♖a8 46 ♕e4!

At last White has it all under control. Now his threats include 47 b5 and 47 f5. Black can only sacrifice the exchange back, but the resulting queen and pawn endgame is hopeless.

46...♕a2 47 ♕xc6 ♖xa7 48 ♗xa7 ♕xa7+ 49 ♕c5 ♕a2 50 ♕c8+ ♚h7 51 ♕f5+ ♚g8 52 ♕e4 ♕d2 53 e6 ♕d1+ 54 ♚f2 ♕d2+ 55 ♚g3 ♕d1 56 e7 ♕g1+ 57 ♚h3 ♕f1+ 58 ♚g4 h5+ 59 ♚xh5 1-0

An eventful clash. Although extremely complex, White seems to have the upper hand after 11 ♘b5. Consequently, Black should consider preventing this with 10...a6 or 10...c6.

Game 62
Svidler-Terekhin
St Petersburg Open 1994

1 e4 d5 2 exd5 ♘f6 3 ♗b5+ ♗d7 4 ♗e2

4 ♗xd7+ should not cause Black any concern. After 4...♕xd7 5 c4 c6! 6 dxc6 ♘xc6 7 ♘f3 e5 8 0-0 ♗c5 (or 8...e4!?) Black has tremendous compensation for the pawn.

4...♘xd5 5 d4 ♗f5 6 ♘f3 e6 7 0-0 ♗e7 8 a3

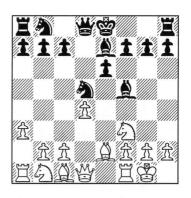

8...0-0 9 c4 ♘b6

The most common choice, but naturally 9...♘f6 is a playable alternative. In Kroeze-Van Tol, Holland 1995, White achieved an advantage after 10 ♘c3 ♘bd7 11 ♗f4 c5?! 12 d5 exd5 13 cxd5 ♘e4 14 d6 ♗f6 15 ♕d5. However, Black should probably play the simplifying 10...♘e4 or 11...♘e4, as an exchange of minor pieces will ease his slightly cramped position.

10 ♘c3 ♘c6 11 ♗e3 ♗f6 12 b3 ♕e7!

Superficially White's centre looks quite impressive, but with 12...♕e7 Black plans the simple ...♖ad8 and ...e6-e5, when White may begin to feel the strain. Svidler side-stepped this with his next move, but the resulting structure is also absolutely okay for Black.

13 c5 ♘d5 14 ♘xd5 exd5 15 b4

White hopes to cramp his opponent on the queen's wing, before the slight weakness of the pawn on d4 begins to tell.

15...a6 16 ♖e1 ♖fe8 17 ♕d2 ♗e4 18 h3 h6 19 a4

see following diagram

19...a5!

Securing the b4-outpost for the knight. After this Black has fully equalised.

20 b5 ♘b4 21 ♖ac1 ♗xf3 22 ♗xf3

♗g5 23 ♗g4 ♕f6 24 ♗d7 ♖e4 25 ♗xg5 ♕xg5 26 ♕xg5 ♖xe1+ 27 ♖xe1 hxg5 28 b6

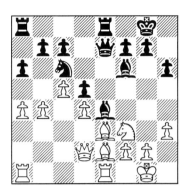

This leads to a drawn position. Notice that 28 ♖e7 leads nowhere after 28...♔f8.

28...cxb6 29 cxb6 ♖a6 30 ♖e8+ ♔h7 31 ♖e7 ♖xb6

The safest choice. Not, however, 31...f6 32 ♗f5+ ♔h6 33 ♖xb7 or 31...♔g6 32 ♗e8 ♖xb6 33 ♖xf7, both of which favour White.

32 ♖xf7 ♖f6 33 ♖e7 ♘c6 34 ♗xc6 bxc6 35 ♖e3 ♖f7

Intending ...♖b7-b4. White secures a draw via a repetition of moves.

36 ♖c3 ♖f4 37 ♖d3 ♖f7 ½-½

Game 63
Vlassov-Terekhin
St Petersburg Open 1994

1 e4 d5 2 exd5 ♘f6 3 ♗b5+ ♗d7 4 ♗c4 ♗g4 5 f3

The quiet 5 ♘f3 is the subject of Game 67.

5...♗c8

5...♗f5 will be discussed in Games 65 and 66. After 5...♗c8 Black's bishop has made three consecutive moves only to wind up on its original square. However, White has also lost some time, as well as having had to play the 'ugly' f2-f3.

6 ♘c3 ♘bd7 7 ♕e2!?

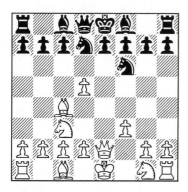

The most ambitious try. White keeps hold of the extra pawn at all costs. The sensible 7 d4 will be studied in the next game.

7...♘b6 8 ♕d3 g6 9 ♗b3?!

This, together with 10 ♕b5+ and 11 ♘e4, seems rather excessive. I prefer the straightforward 9 ♘ge2.

9...♗g7 10 ♕b5+ ♘bd7! 11 ♘e4 0-0 12 ♘e2 a6 13 ♕b4 ♘b6 14 ♘xf6+ ♗xf6 15 ♕a5 ♖e8 16 0-0 e6!

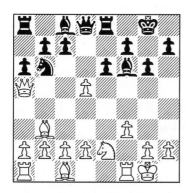

So White has managed to maintain the pawn plus, but that is only half the story. With 16...e6! the position explodes and White's lack of development proves to be fatal.

17 ♘f4

17 dxe6 ♗xe6 18 ♗xe6 ♖xe6 also leaves Black with an awesome position. One possible finish would be 19 ♘c3 ♕d4+ 20 ♔h1 ♕f2!

17...♗d4+ 18 ♔h1 exd5 19 ♘xd5 ♕h4

The many threats are becoming more than just irritating. First, White has to prevent the simple ...♖e1.

20 d3 ♖e5!

Now the decisive ...♖h5 is in the air. White tries to steal some time by attacking the black queen, but instead he allows a very publishable finish.

21 g3

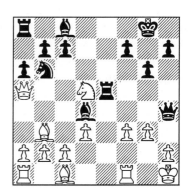

21...♕xh2+!! 22 ♔xh2 ♖h5+ 23 ♔g2 ♗h3+ 24 ♔h2 ♗xf1 mate 0-1

A significant warning to White players in this line. Take liberties and you will be punished!

Game 64
Suetin-Bachmann
Berlin Open 1992

1 e4 d5 2 exd5 ♘f6 3 ♗b5+ ♗d7 4

♗c4 ♗g4 5 f3 ♗c8 6 ♘c3 ♘bd7 7 d4 ♘b6 8 ♕d3!?

An new interesting idea; formerly 8 ♗b3 was the most popular move here. The 3 ♗b5+ variation was contested four times in the Women's World Championship battle between Alexandria and Gaprindashvili in 1975, with Black (Gaprindashvili) scoring a highly commendable 3/4. The first of the four encounters continued 8 ♗b3 ♘bxd5 9 ♘xd5 ♘xd5 10 c4 ♘f6 11 ♗e3 c6 (11...e6 may be stronger, intending classical development with 12 ♘e2 ♗e7 13 0-0 0-0) 12 ♕d2 g6 13 ♘e2 ♗g7 14 0-0 0-0 15 ♖ad1 b5 16 cxb5 cxb5 17 d5!, and White had an edge, although Gaprindashvili eventually won.

8...♘bxd5 9 ♘xd5 ♘xd5 10 ♗d2 g6

In hindsight, perhaps Black should opt for the restrained 10...e6, followed by ...♗e7 and ...0-0.

11 ♘e2 ♗g7 12 h4! h5

No doubt after 12...0-0 Suetin's intention would have been 13 h5!, with an ominous looking attack.

13 ♗g5 c6 14 ♕d2 ♗f5 15 a3 ♕d7 16 ♗b3 ♗e6 17 c4 ♘b6 18 ♕b4 ♘c8?

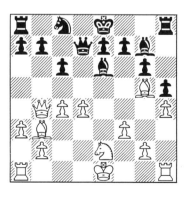

I don't like this move at all. Black had to 'bite the bullet' with 18...0-0. White has no immediate attack and 19 ♗xe7 ♖fe8 allows Black some unwelcome counterplay.

19 0-0-0 ♘d6 20 ♔b1 0-0-0 21 ♔a1 ♗h6 22 ♗xh6 ♖xh6 23 d5!

With Black's rook temporarily misplaced on h6, White seizes the chance to open the position in the centre, with decisive consequences.

23...cxd5 24 cxd5 ♗f5 25 ♘d4!

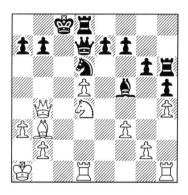

25...♔b8

This move, giving up the exchange, is the equivalent of resignation, but 25...♖f8 26 ♖c1+ ♔b8 27 ♗a4 is absolutely crushing.

26 ♘c6+ ♔a8 27 ♘xd8 ♕xd8 28 ♖he1 ♖h8 29 ♖e3 ♗d7 30 ♖c1 ♖e8 31 ♖ec3 a6 32 a4 ♔a7 33 ♖c7 ♔b8 34 ♕a5 ♗c6 35 ♖1xc6 1-0

Game 65
Alexandria-Gaprindashvili
Women's World Ch, Tbilisi 1975

---

1 e4 d5 2 exd5 ♘f6 3 ♗b5+ ♗d7 4 ♗c4 ♗g4 5 f3 ♗f5 6 g4

Forcing the bishop back to base, but at a visible cost of loosening the kingside pawns. The prudent 6 ♘c3 is considered in Game 66.

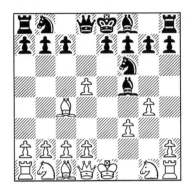

6...♗c8 7 ♘c3 c6!

The most consistent policy against White's play. 7...♘bd7 sees one of the positive points of 6 g4: after 8 g5! ♘h5 9 d3 White keeps the extra pawn with a clear plus.

8 dxc6 ♘xc6 9 d3 e5 10 g5

This is extremely committal. I prefer 10 ♗e3, with the plain idea of ♘ge2, ♕d2 and possibly 0-0-0.

10...♘h5 11 ♘e4 ♗e7 12 ♘e2 0-0 13 c3

Again 13 ♗e3 looks stronger.

13...♘a5! 14 ♗e3 ♘xc4 15 dxc4 ♕c7

The outcome of the opening moves

has not been agreeable for White. The lead in development, bishop pair and healthier pawn structure give Black more than enough compensation for the pawn.

16 b3 ♗h3 17 ♖g1 ♖ad8 18 ♕c2 ♔h8 19 ♖d1 ♖xd1+ 20 ♔xd1 ♕d7+ 21 ♔c1 ♕f5! 22 ♘d2 ♗a3+ 23 ♔b1 ♖d8 24 ♘g3

Unfortunately White cannot even trade queens: 24 ♕xf5 ♗xf5+ 25 ♔a1 ♖d3 wins material, as 26 ♘f1 allows 26...♖d1+.

24...♘xg3 25 ♖xg3 b6!

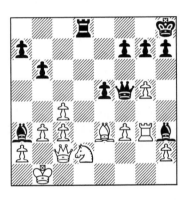

This calm move illustrates Black's superiority. White can barely move.

26 ♖g1

Losing a piece, but it is already becoming difficult to find an alternative:

a) 26 ♕xf5 loses to 26...♗xf5+ 27 ♔a1 (27 ♘e4 ♖d3 28 ♗f2 ♖xf3! 29 ♖xf3 ♗xe4+ and ...♗xf3) 27...♖d3 28 f4 ♗c1! 29 ♘f1 exf4.

b) 26 ♘e4 ♗f1! (threatening ...♗d3) 27 ♘f2 ♖d1+! 28 ♘xd1 ♗d3 and the queen is lost.

26...♗c5! 27 ♗xc5 ♖xd2 28 ♕xf5 ♗xf5+ 29 ♔c1 ♖c2+ 30 ♔d1 bxc5 31 ♖e1 f6 32 f4 ♖xa2 33 gxf6 gxf6 0-1

Game 66
Arning-Holzhaeuer
Correspondence 1986

1 e4 d5 2 exd5 ♘f6 3 ♗b5+ ♗d7 4 ♗c4 ♗g4 5 f3 ♗f5 6 ♘c3 ♘bd7

The speculative gambit 6...c6 is also possible.

7 ♕e2

Once more this is the most dangerous move, dangerous that is for both sides. The rational option is to off-load the extra pawn with 7 ♘ge2 ♘b6 8 ♗b3 (or 8 d3 ♘bxd5 9 ♘xd5 ♘xd5 10 ♘g3) 8...♘bxd5 9 ♘xd5 ♘xd5 10 ♘g3 ♗g6 11 0-0 e6, although Black should be fine here.

7...♘b6 8 ♗b3 ♕d7

An essential precaution as the immediate 8...♘bxd5 allows 9 ♘xd5 ♘xd5 10 ♕b5+ and 11 ♕xb7.

9 d6!? ♕xd6

After 9...cxd6 10 a4 a5 11 ♕e3! ♖a6 12 d3 d5 13 ♘ge2 Black's pieces are placed rather awkwardly.

10 ♘b5 ♕d7 11 ♕e5 0-0-0 12 ♘xa7+ ♔b8 13 ♘b5

White's mini knight tour has netted a pawn, albeit the quite insignificant a-pawn.

13...♘fd5 14 a4 f6

Black certainly has some compensation, but perhaps the way forward is with 14...e6!? 15 ♘e2 f6 (forcing the queen to an inferior square, as the knight has occupied e2) 16 ♕g3 ♘b4 17 ♘ed4 ♗c5 18 ♘xf5 exf5, when the white king may become stranded in the centre.

15 ♕e2 e5 16 a5 ♘f4??

This was supposed to be a significant improvement for Black, but unfortunately it contains a colossal tactical flaw. 16...♘c8 is necessary.

17 axb6 ♘xe2 18 bxc7+??

After 18 ♘xc7! the threat of ♖a8 mate forces 18...♕xc7 19 bxc7+ ♔xc7 20 ♘xe2, when Black can resign.

18...♕xc7 19 ♘xc7 ♘d4!

This is the idea. Despite his extra piece White is clearly worse, as the knight on c7 has to hop into the corner.

20 ♘a8 ♗xc2! 21 ♗c4 b5 22 ♗e2 ♘b3 0-1

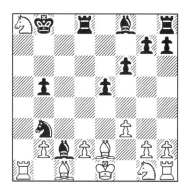

After 22...♘b3 23 ♖a6 ♘xc1 24 ♗xb5 ♗d3! 25 ♗xd3 ♘xd3+ 26 ♔e2 ♘f4+ 27 ♔f1 ♔b7 Black goes from being a piece down to a piece up in

just four moves. All very nice, but 18 ♘xc7 puts a hefty spanner into the works. That said, Black probably has enough for the pawn after 14...e6.

Game 67
Tseshkovsky-Prokopchuk
Kazan 1995

---

1 e4 d5 2 exd5 ♘f6 3 ♗b5+ ♗d7 4 ♗c4 ♗g4 5 ♘f3

This natural move is extremely uncommon in this position, but it is by no means bad.

5...♘xd5 6 c3!?

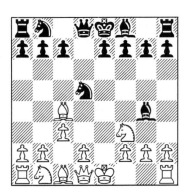

A new idea. White cleverly defers d2-d4 and opens an avenue for the queen, which may suddenly appear on b3 or a4. Black has to be extremely careful with his next move.

6...c6

Other moves fall foul of White's cunning 6 c3:

a) 6...♘b6? and 6...♘f6? both run into 7 ♗xf7+ ♔xf7 8 ♘e5+.

b) 6...e6? 7 ♕a4+ ♕d7 (or 7...c6? 8 ♗xd5 and 9 ♕xg4) 8 ♗b5 c6 9 ♗xc6 ♘xc6 10 ♕xg4 and White has an extra pawn.

c) 6...♘c6?! 7 ♕b3 ♗xf3 (7...♘a5 8

♕a4+ c6 9 ♗xd5 wins) 8 ♕xb7! ♘b6 (8...♘a5? 9 ♗b5+ c6 10 ♗xc6+ ♘xc6 11 ♕xc6+ ♕d7 12 ♕xa8+) 9 gxf3 ♘e5 10 ♗b5+ ♘ed7 11 d4, again with a healthy pawn advantage.

d) 6...g6?! 7 ♕b3 ♗xf3 8 gxf3 and the b-pawn drops.

7 d4 e6 8 ♘bd2 ♘d7 9 h3 ♗f5 10 0-0 ♗e7 11 ♖e1 0-0 12 ♘e4 ♕c7 13 ♗d3 b5 14 ♗d2 ♗g6 15 ♕b1 ♖ab8 16 ♘eg5 ♗xd3 17 ♕xd3 ♗xg5 18 ♘xg5 ♘7f6 19 a4 a6

Not 19...bxa4?! 20 c4 ♘e7 21 ♗c3, when the a4-pawn would soon drop, leaving the rest of Black's queenside pawns in a sorry state.

20 ♘e4 ♘xe4 21 ♖xe4 ♖bd8 22 ♗g5 ♖d7 23 axb5 axb5 24 ♕f3 ♘e7

Tseshkovsky had been trying to drum up a kingside attack with ♖h4 and ♕h5, so Black takes the necessary precautions. The position is finely balanced. White can continue to irritate Black with threats on the kingside, but if Black were able to exchange some major pieces, then the position may even turn out to be favourable for him. White must be careful not to end up with a 'bad' bishop scenario.

25 ♗f4 ♕b7 26 h4!

Launching the h-pawn in order to soften up Black's pawn structure.

26...♖d5 27 h5 ♖f5 28 ♕g4 g6 29 hxg6 hxg6

---

see following diagram

---

30 ♗e5?

In his annotations to the game, Bangiev suggests the powerful 30 ♗d6!, with the following lines:

a) 30...♖h5? 31 ♖xe6! fxe6

(31...♕d7? 32 ♖xg6+) 32 ♗xe7 ♕xe7 33 ♕xg6+ and White regains the rook with a winning position.

b) 30...♖e8 31 ♗c5 ♕c8 32 ♖a7 ♘d5 33 ♕g3 with a strong initiative.

30...♖h5! 31 ♕f3?

Continuing to err. 31 ♗f6, playing on the weak dark squares, would have been more effective. Now Black is able to take over operations.

31...f5! 32 ♖ee1 ♘d5

Black has seized the h-file and suddenly White is faced with threats such as 33...♕h7.

33 ♗d6 ♖e8 34 ♕g3 ♕h7 35 f3 g5 36 ♗e5

White also goes down after 36 ♔f2 f4 37 ♕g4 ♘f6!, trapping the queen.

36...f4 37 ♗xf4

A regretful move, but 37 ♕g4 ♘e3 38 ♖xe3 ♖h1+ 39 ♔f2 fxe3+ is no better.

37...♘xf4 38 ♖e5 ♖h1+ 39 ♔f2 ♕c2+ 0-1

It is mate next move. A Black victory in the end, but 5 ♘f3 and 6 c3 looks well worth a try.

> ### Game 68
> ### Tseshkovsky-Naumkin
> *USSR 1987*

1 e4 d5 2 exd5 ♘f6 3 ♗b5+ ♗d7 4 ♗c4 b5

This is another acceptable method for Black. The bishop is driven away, while space is gained on the queenside.

5 ♗b3 a5 6 a4

After 6 a3 Black should revert to the usual lines with 6...♗g4 7 f3 ♗c8. Malysev-Smagin, Correspondence 1984, continued 8 ♘c3 ♗a6! 9 ♘ge2 g6 10 ♘d4 ♕d7 11 ♕e2 a4 12 ♗a2 b4 13 ♘cb5 b3 14 cxb3 axb3 15 ♗xb3 ♗g7 and White's knights were in a tangle.

6...bxa4 7 ♗a2!?

7 ♗xa4 ♘xd5 looks equal.

7...♗g4! 8 f3 ♗c8 9 ♘c3

After 9 c4 Black should not hesitate to play 9...c6! 10 dxc6 ♘xc6, with the usual compensation. White decides to return the pawn and an even position is reached.

9...♗b7 10 ♘ge2 ♘xd5 11 ♘xd5 ♗xd5 12 ♗xd5 ♕xd5 13 ♖xa4 ♘d7 14 0-0 e6

see following diagram

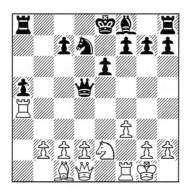

15 ♘c3 ♕c6 16 ♕e2 ♗b4 17 ♕b5 ♕b6+!? 18 ♕xb6 ♘xb6 19 ♖a2 a4 20 ♘e4 ♚d7 21 ♖d1 h6 ½-½

Game 69
Schumacher-Yewdokimow
Correspondence 1954

1 e4 d5 2 exd5 ♘f6 3 ♗b5+ ♘bd7

This move is less popular than 3...♗d7, but it does offer Black some attractive possibilities.

4 c4 a6 5 ♗xd7+

After 5 ♗a4 Black carries on in gambit fashion with 5...b5! 6 cxb5 ♘xd5. Canfell-Dunnington, Oakham 1988, ran 7 ♘c3 ♘5b6! 8 ♗b3 axb5 9 d4 (9 ♘xb5 ♗a6 10 ♘c3 ♘c5 is very irritating for White) 9...b4 10 ♘e4 e6 11 ♘e2 ♗b7 12 ♕c2 c5 13 dxc5 ♗xe4 14 ♕xe4 ♘xc5 15 ♕f3 ♘xb3 16 ♕xb3 ♕d5 17 ♕xd5 ♘xd5 18 0-0 ♗d6, and Black had a small endgame edge.

5...♕xd7!

An important capture. After 5...♗xd7 6 d4 b5 7 b3 e6 8 dxe6 ♗xe6 9 d5 ♗g4 10 f3 ♗f5 11 ♘e2 ♗c5 12 ♗b2 ♕e7 13 ♗d4 ♗xd4 14 ♕xd4 0-0 15 ♔f2 ♖ad8 16 ♘bc3 b4 17 ♘g3! Black had no compensation in Anand-

Galego, Oviedo (rapidplay) 1993.
6 d3 b5

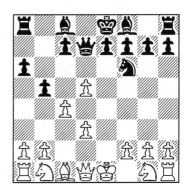

Also possible are 6...c6!? and 6...e6!?
7 ♕e2?

There is no need to bring the queen out so early. Development with 7 ♘f3 looks much more sensible.

7...bxc4 8 dxc4 c6! 9 dxc6 ♕xc6 10 ♘f3 ♗b7 11 ♘a3?! 0-0-0 12 ♘c2 e5 13 0-0 ♗d6 14 ♖d1 ♘g4 15 ♘e3 ♘xe3 16 fxe3? h5 17 ♗d2 h4 18 h3 g5 19 ♖f1 g4 20 hxg4 h3 21 ♖f2 hxg2 0-1

After 22 ♔xg2 ♖dg8 Black's attack would be overwhelming.

So Black can obtain good chances with 3...♘bd7, although White's play in this game was pretty dreadful.

Summary

It seems that Black has quite a few satisfactory ideas against 3 ♗b5+, which is probably the reason for its decline over the past few years. After 3...♗d7 4 ♗c4, both 4...b5 and 4...♗g4 have yielded good results for the second player, so much so that White players have been changing to the restrained 4 ♗e2. 3...♘bd7 still requires further tests but everything points to this being yet another adequate defence.

1 e4 d5 2 exd5 ♘f6 3 ♗b5+

3...♗d7
     3...♘bd7 - *game 69*
4 ♗e2 *(D)*
     4 ♗c4
          4...♗g4 *(D)*
               5 f3
                    5...♗c8 6 ♘c3 ♘bd7
                         7 ♕e2 - *game 63*
                         7 d4 - *game 64*
                    5...♗f5
                         6 g4 - *game 65*
                         6 ♘c3 - *game 66*
             5 ♘f3 - *game 67*
          4...b5 - *game 68*
4...♘xd5 5 d4 ♗f5 6 ♘f3 e6 7 0-0 ♗e7 *(D)*
     8 c4 - *game 61*
     8 a3 - *game 62*

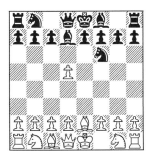
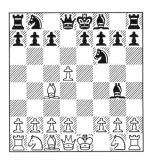

| 4 ♗e2 | 4...♗g4 | 7...♗e7 |

CHAPTER TEN

2...♘f6: Scandinavian Gambit and Panov Attack

1 e4 d5 2 exd5 ♘f6 3 c4 c6

3 c4 is another important response to 2...♘f6. Black is virtually forced to sacrifice a pawn with either 3...e6 (see Chapter 11) or 3...c6. After 3...c6 4 dxc6 ♘xc6 nobody can argue about Black's compensation. Indeed, this line is seen quite infrequently. Even though White's position is playable, not many players are willing to give up the initiative and accept structural weaknesses at such an early juncture.

White's main response to 3...c6 is to transpose to the Caro-Kann, Panov-Botvinnik Attack with 4 d4 cxd5 5 ♘c3 (or alternatively 4 ♘c3 cxd5 5 d4). 4 ♘c3 cxd5 5 cxd5 ♘xd5 is also sometimes played, but this generally transposes to one of the main lines of the Panov. Strictly speaking all of these variations belong to the Caro-Kann, and therefore should lie outside the scope of this book. In any case, to give these lines the attention they really deserve would take a whole publication in itself. Nevertheless, in order to give Black players an overview of the ideas, I have decided to give a brief summary of the latest theoretical wrinkles, concentrating on the absolute main lines.

After 1 e4 d5 2 exd5 ♘f6 3 c4 c6 4 d4 cxd5 5 ♘c3 Black has three main choices: 5...e6, 5...♘c6 and 5...g6. Of these, 5...e6 is the most solid option, and a great favourite of FIDE Champion Anatoly Karpov. Normally a typical isolated d-pawn position is reached early on. White aims to play actively, creating threats in the centre and against the black king. In return Black often tries to exchange pieces, relieving the tension and increasing the importance of the weakness of White's d4-pawn. These types of position have been debated for decades and there are still no real conclusions.

5...♘c6 is a trickier move, which can either lead to extremely complex play or a technical endgame. Current opinion seems to suggest that Black is holding his own in both of these lines.

5...g6 has been reasonably accepted in the past. Over the years, however, more than one way has been discovered to give White at least a small edge and its popularity has gradually waned. In the late 1980s the English Grandmaster Keith Arkell was one of its main practitioners, but even he is starting to favour the more orthodox 5...e6.

Game 70
Chandler-Adams
Hastings 1989/90

1 e4 d5 2 exd5 ♘f6 3 c4 c6 4 dxc6

A miserly pawn-grab. Black is bound to have sufficient compensation, particularly as the squares d4 and d3 are so vulnerable. As a result 4 dxc6 is witnessed only very rarely at the highest levels and I imagine that even this game was simply an attempt by Chandler to get Adams into uncharted territory.

4...♘xc6 5 ♘f3 e5 6 d3 e4!

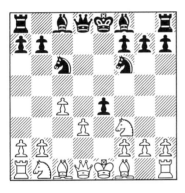

Naturally the straightforward 6...♗c5 and 6...♗f5 are also fully playable. In those cases Black would develop normally before applying pressure to White's position, particularly the insecure d3-pawn. Nevertheless, 6...e4 is the simplest method to achieve a satisfactory position.

7 dxe4

As one would expect, 7 ♕e2? is dealt with a swift refutation. 7...♗b4+ 8 ♗d2 0-0 9 dxe4 ♘xe4 10 ♗xb4 ♖e8! and a simple knight retreat will pick up the queen.

7...♕xd1+ 8 ♔xd1 ♘xe4 9 ♗e3 ♗f5 10 ♘h4 0-0-0+ 11 ♔c1

The optimistic 11 ♔e2 came to a sticky end in Holzmann-Kaspar, Correspondence 1980. That miniature ended with 11...♗e6 12 ♔f3 (12 b3 g5 13 ♘f3 ♗g7 is embarrassing) 12...f5 13 g4 ♘e5+ 14 ♔f4 g5+! 15 ♔xe5 ♗d6+ 16 ♔d4 (16 ♔xe6 ♖he8+ also leads to mate after 17 ♔xf5 ♖e5 or 17 ♔f7 ♖e7 mate) 16...♗c7 mate.

11...♗e6 12 ♘c3 ♘xc3 13 bxc3 b6 14 ♘f3 ♗c5 15 ♗xc5 bxc5

Summing up, we see that Black has remained active while White's 'extra' pawn has become totally insignificant. So it is White who is trying to equalise.

16 ♖b1 ♖he8 17 ♗e2 ♗h3!

This gives Black a clear edge in the endgame, which Adams was ultimately able to convert into the full point.

18 gxh3 ♖xe2 19 ♖b2 ♖xb2 20 ♔xb2 ♖d3 21 ♘g5 ♖d2+ 22 ♔a3 ♖xf2 23 ♖d1 h6 24 ♘e4 ♖xh2 25 ♖g1 ♖e2 26 ♘xc5 g6 27 ♖g3 ♘e5 28 ♔b3 ♔c7 29 ♘a6+ ♔b6 30 ♘b4 ♖e4 31 ♖g1 a5 32 ♘d5+ ♔c5 33 ♖d1 ♘xc4 34 ♘f6 ♖f4 35 ♘d7+

♔c6 36 a4 g5 37 ♘b8+ ♔c7 38
♘d7 ♘d6 39 ♘e5 ♖f5 40 ♘g4 h5
41 ♘e3 ♖f3 42 ♘d5+ ♔c6 43 h4
gxh4 44 ♘e7+ ♔d7 45 ♘c8 ♔xc8
46 ♖xd6 h3 47 ♖d4 h2 48 ♖h4 ♖f2
49 ♖xh5 f5 50 ♔c4 ♖d2 51 ♔c5 f4
52 ♔c6 ♔d8 53 c4 f3 54 c5 ♖g2 55
♔b6 ♖b2+ 56 ♔c6 f2 0-1

White decides to call it a day as 57
♖xh2 f1♕ 58 ♖xb2 ♕f6+ picks up the
rook.

> ### Game 71
> ### Adams-Morovic Fernandez
> *Leon 1995*

**1 e4 c6 2 d4 d5 3 exd5 cxd5 4 c4
♘f6 5 ♘c3 ♘c6 6 ♘f3**

The alternative 6 ♗g5 is considered
in the next game.

**6...♗g4 7 cxd5 ♘xd5 8 ♕b3 ♗xf3 9
gxf3 e6**

This is the sensible approach. The
main alternative 9...♘b6 is much
more hazardous, and can lead to crazy
complications after 10 d5 (if White
does not fancy entering a tactical
maze, then the safer 10 ♗e3 should be
chosen) 10...♘d4 11 ♕d1 e5 12 dxe6
fxe6 13 ♗e3 ♗c5 14 b4 ♕f6! 15 bxc5
♘xf3+ 16 ♔e2 0-0 17 cxb6 ♖ad8. One
recent example continued 18 ♕c2
♘d4+ 19 ♗xd4 ♕xd4 20 ♘e4 ♕xa1
21 ♗g2 ♕e5 22 bxa7!? ♕b5+ 23 ♔e3
♕a6 24 ♖b1 ♕xa7+ 25 ♔e2 ♖c8 26
♕b3 ♕a6+, and the players called a
truce, although there was still plenty
to play for in the final position in
Rozentalis-B.Lalic, Moscow Olympiad 1994.

**10 ♕xb7 ♘xd4 11 ♗b5+ ♘xb5 12
♕c6+ ♔e7 13 ♕xb5 ♕d7 14 ♘xd5+**

♕xd5 15 ♕xd5 exd5

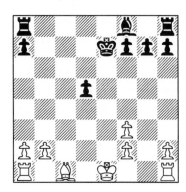

This position has been reached sev-
eral times at master level. The general
consensus is that White holds a
minimal advantage, but with accurate
play Black should be okay. It has to
be said that the majority of games
starting from this position do wind up
as draws, and this one proves to be no
exception.

**16 0-0 ♔e6 17 ♖e1+ ♔f5 18 ♖d1
♖d8 19 ♗e3 ♖d7 20 ♖d4 ♗c5 21
♖f4+ ♔e5 22 ♖c1 ♗xe3 23 fxe3
♖b8 24 b3 ♖bb7 25 ♔f2 ♖bc7 26
♖xc7 ♖xc7 27 ♖a4 ♔d6 28 h4 ♔c5
29 ♔g3 ♔b6 30 ♖b4+ ♔c5 31 ♖a4
♔b6 32 ♖d4 ♔c6 33 ♔f4 ♖e7 34
♖b4 h6 35 e4 dxe4 36 fxe4 ♖e6 37
♖c4+ ♔b7 38 ♖c5 ♖a6 39 ♖f5 f6 40
♖b5+ ♔c7 41 a4 g5+ 42 hxg5
hxg5+ 43 ♔f5 ♖b6 44 ♖c5+ ♖c6 45
♖a5**

see following diagram

45 ♖xc6+ seems to be a better try,
although after 45...♔xc6 46 ♔xf6 g4
47 e5 g3 48 e6 g2 49 e7 g1♕ 50 e8♕+
♔b6 Black should still be able to hold.

**45...a6 46 b4 ♖b6 47 ♖c5+ ♖c6 48
♖a5 ½-½**

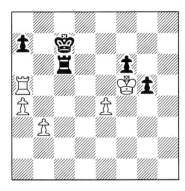

1 e4 c6 2 d4 d5 3 exd5 cxd5 4 c4 ♘f6 5 ♘c3 ♘c6 6 ♗g5 ♗e6

This bizarre looking move is currently thought to be the most challenging reply to 6 ♗g5. On e6 the bishop commits the 'cardinal sin' of blocking e-pawn. Nevertheless, it does add pressure against White's centre and the dark-squared bishop can always be fianchettoed. Other reasonable responses are 6...e6, 6...dxc4 and 6...♕a5.

7 a3!?

The idea of this move is to discourage ...♕a5, which is one of Black's chief ideas in the 6...♗e6 line. Now, of course, 7...♕a5 may be answered simply by 8 b4. Other possibilities include 7 ♗xf6, 7 ♘ge2, 7 g3 and 7 c5. A wild game Rogers-Dreev, Biel 1993, went 7 ♗e2 ♕a5 8 ♘f3 dxc4 9 0-0 ♖d8 10 ♕c1 h6 11 ♗d2 ♘xd4! 12 ♘xd4 ♖xd4 13 b4! ♕d8 14 ♗e3 ♖d7, and now White's best is 15 ♗xa7 g5 16 ♘b5, with an unclear position.

7...♕d7 8 ♗xf6 gxf6 9 g3?!

In his notes to the game, Leko criticises this move and then admits that he can hardly find anything better for White! 9 b4 suggests itself, but in any case Black has good counter-chances.

9...0-0-0 10 ♗g2

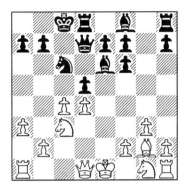

10...♗g4! 11 f3 ♗e6

Black has expended two tempi to induce White to block the diagonal with f2-f3. No doubt 12 f4 would have been answered by 12...♗g4!

12 c5 ♗f5 13 b4 e5 14 ♘ge2 ♕e6

Black's control of the centre and lead in development already gives him an advantage of significant proportions. Theoretically this game is a fantastic success for Black.

15 dxe5 d4 16 ♘e4 d3 17 ♘f4 d2+ 18 ♔f2 ♕c4! 19 ♗h3 ♗xh3 20 ♘xh3 ♕d4+ 21 ♔g2 ♘xe5 22 ♕b3 ♘c4 23 ♖hd1 f5 24 ♘eg5 ♖d7 25 f4 ♗g7 26 ♘f2 ♕d5+ 27 ♘f3 ♗xa1 28 ♖xa1 ♖e8 0-1

1 e4 c6 2 d4 d5 3 exd5 cxd5 4 c4

♘f6 5 ♘c3 e6 6 ♘f3 ♗e7

The alternative 6...♗b4 is considered in the next game.

7 cxd5 ♘xd5 8 ♗d3 ♘c6 9 0-0 0-0 10 ♖e1 ♗f6 11 ♗e4 ♘ce7

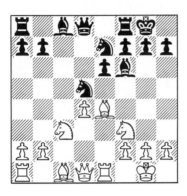

A critical juncture. White has two main tries for the advantage.

12 ♕d3

Ivanchuk-Karpov, Roquebrune 1992, continued instead 12 ♘e5 ♗d7 (12...♘c6!? is also okay for Black) 13 ♕d3 ♘g6 14 ♗d2 ♗c6 15 ♘xc6 bxc6 16 ♘a4 ♘b6 17 ♘xb6 ♕xb6 18 ♗e3 ♖ad8 with an equal game.

12...h6 13 ♘e5 ♘xc3 14 ♕xc3 ♘f5 15 ♗e3 a5!?

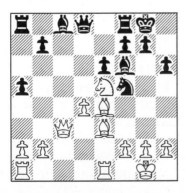

16 ♖ac1 a4 17 ♖ed1 ♘xe3 18 ♕xe3 ♕b6 19 ♘g4 ♗g5 20 f4 ♗e7 21

♗b1 ♗d7 22 ♕g3! f5! 23 ♘xh6+ ♔h7 24 ♘g4 ♖fd8 25 ♘e5 ♗e8

Pressure on b2 and d4 gives Black some compensation for the pawn deficit.

26 ♕e3 ♗f6 27 g4?!

This is the first in a series minor inaccuracies by White. Ftacnik recommends the simple 27 ♖d2, when White maintains an edge.

27...g6 28 gxf5 exf5 29 ♕c3?! ♖ac8 30 ♕h3+

Or 30 ♕xc8 ♖xc8 31 ♖xc8 ♗c6 with an unclear position.

30...♔g7 31 ♖xc8 ♖xc8 32 ♕g2 ♖d8 33 ♕f2 ♗e7 34 h4? ♕f6! 35 ♖c1 ♕xh4 36 ♖c7 ♔f8 37 ♕e3?! ♗d6 38 ♖xb7 ♗xe5 39 ♕xe5 ♕g3+ 40 ♔f1 ♕f3+ 41 ♔e1 ♕xb7 42 ♕f6+ ♗f7 43 ♕xd8+ ♔g7

After a flurry of tactics it has suddenly become quite obvious that White is in serious trouble due to his severely draughty king.

44 d5 ♕b4+ 45 ♔d1 ♕d4+ 46 ♔c2 ♕e4+ 47 ♔c3

Fatally dropping the bishop, although 47 ♔c1 ♕xf4+ 48 ♔d1 ♕d4+ 49 ♔c1 ♗xd5 also wins for Black.

47...♕xb1 48 d6 ♕e1+ 49 ♔d4

♕b4+ 50 ♔e3

50 ♔e5 allows the pretty 50...♕xb2 mate.

50...♕e4+ 51 ♔d2 ♕xf4+ 52 ♔c2 ♕e4+ 53 ♔d2 ♕d4+ 54 ♔c1 f4 0-1

Ftacnik gives the variation 54...f4 55 d7 f3 56 ♕e7 f2 57 d8♕ f1♕+ 58 ♔c2 ♕fd3+ 59 ♔c1 ♕d1 mate.

Game 74
Hebden-Arkell
Hastings Masters 1995

---

1 e4 c6 2 d4 d5 3 exd5 cxd5 4 c4 ♘f6 5 ♘c3 e6 6 ♘f3 ♗b4 7 cxd5

7 ♗d3 is an important alternative to the text. After 7...dxc4 8 ♗xc4 0-0 9 0-0 we have actually transposed to a well-known line of the Nimzo-Indian Defence (1 d4 ♘f6 2 c4 e6 3 ♘c3 ♗b4 4 e3 0-0 5 ♗d3 d5 6 ♘f3 c5 7 0-0 cxd4 8 exd4 dxc4 9 ♗xc4).

7...♘xd5 8 ♗d2

8 ♕c2 introduces an interesting pawn sacrifice, which has had some extensive tests at master level. After 8...♘c6 9 a3 ♗a5 10 ♗d3 ♘xc3!? 11 bxc3 ♘xd4 12 ♘xd4 ♕xd4 13 ♗b5+ ♗d7 14 0-0 White obtains a dangerous attack.

8...♘c6 9 ♗d3 0-0 10 0-0 ♗e7 11 ♕e2 ♗f6 12 ♖ad1

see following diagram

12...b6

Black would like to grab the d-pawn, but this looks too hazardous to me. After 12...♘xd4 13 ♘xd4 ♗xd4 14 ♘xd5! Black has a choice of two evils:

a) 14...exd5 15 ♗b4! ♖e8 16 ♗xh7+ ♔xh7 17 ♕h5+ ♔g8 18 ♖xd4 ♗e6 19

♖h4 with a nasty attack.

b) 14...♕xd5 15 ♗c3! e5 16 ♗xh7+ ♔xh7 17 ♕h5+ ♔g8 18 ♖xd4 ♕e6 19 ♖h4 and again White has the initiative.

13 ♕e4! g6 14 ♗h6 ♗g7 15 ♗xg7 ♔xg7 16 ♘xd5 ♕xd5 17 ♕xd5 exd5 18 ♗b5 ♗b7 19 ♖fe1 ♔f6 20 g4 h6 21 h4 ♖fe8 22 ♗xc6 ♗xc6 23 ♘e5

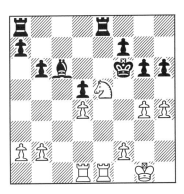

White has a nagging pull as the knight is a better piece than the bishop, which will always be penned in by the d5-pawn. Black will have to suffer long and hard in this endgame.

23...♗b7 24 ♖e3 ♔g7 25 g5 hxg5 26 hxg5 ♖ac8 27 ♖a3 a5 28 ♖dd3 ♖c1+ 29 ♔g2 ♖e7 30 ♖d2 ♗a6 31 ♖e3 ♖ec7 32 ♘g4 ♖a1 33 ♘f6 ♖cc1

34 ♔g3 ♖h1 35 f3 ♖h8 36 ♖e8 ♖xe8 37 ♘xe8+ ♔f8 38 ♘c7 ♗b7 39 ♖e2 ♖c1 40 ♘e8 ♗c6 41 ♘f6 ♖c4 42 b3!

This leads to a very attractive finish.

42...♖xd4 43 ♖c2 ♗b5 44 a4 ♗f1 45 ♖c1! 1-0

Since after 45...♗a6 46 ♖e1 Black can do nothing to prevent ♖e8+ and ♖g8 mate. A triumph on the dark squares!

Game 75
H.Hunt-B.Thipsay
Erevan (Women's Olympiad) 1996

---

1 e4 c6 2 d4 d5 3 exd5 cxd5 4 c4 ♘f6 5 ♘c3 g6

Of Black's three main replies here, 5...g6 has the least respectable reputation. The problem is that White can virtually force the win of the pawn. Although this pawn is doubled and isolated, it often has great nuisance value, as it controls important central squares.

6 ♕b3 ♗g7 7 cxd5 0-0 8 ♗e2 ♘bd7 9 ♗f3 ♘b6 10 ♗g5 a5

Perhaps 10...♗g4 is a more resilient move, although White still keeps a small plus after 11 ♗xf6 ♗xf3 12 ♘xf3 ♗xf6 13 0-0.

11 ♘ge2 a4 12 ♕b5 ♗d7 13 ♕b4 ♗f5 14 0-0

14 d6 also looks good. After 14...exd6 15 ♗xb7 ♖b8 16 ♗f3 ♗d3 17 0-0 ♖e8 18 ♖fe1 h6 19 ♗f4 ♘c4 20 ♕xa4 ♘xb2 21 ♕a3 g5 22 ♗g3 ♘c4

23 ♕c1 ♖c8 24 ♕d1 White was a safe pawn up in Wahls-Graf, Germany 1988.

14...♕d6 15 ♕xd6 exd6

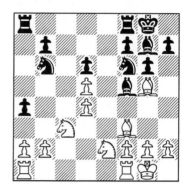

Theoretically speaking this position is supposed to be better for White and I agree with this assessment. In any case Thipsay was always struggling to stay in the game.

16 ♘g3 ♗d3 17 ♖fd1 ♗a6 18 ♘ge4 ♘xe4 19 ♘xe4 ♘c8 20 ♗f4 ♖d8 21 ♖ac1 h6 22 ♖c7 f5 23 ♘g3 ♘b6 24 h4! ♖ac8 25 ♖dc1 ♗f8 26 ♗d2 ♖xc7 27 ♖xc7 ♘a8 28 ♖c1 h5 29 ♘e2

The knight plans to rest on f4. White dominates the whole board and is still a pawn up.

29...♔f7 30 ♘f4 ♖d7 31 ♘e6 ♗e7 32 g3 ♘b6 33 b3 axb3 34 axb3 ♗d3 35 ♗a5 ♘a8 36 ♖c8 b6 37 ♗b4 ♖a7 38 ♘d8+ ♔g7 39 ♘c6 ♖a1+ 40 ♔h2 ♗f8 41 ♖d8 ♗c2 42 ♗xd6 ♗xd6 43 ♖xd6 ♗xb3 44 ♖d7+ 1-0

The passed d5-pawn will become too powerful.

Summary

5...e6, with Karpov's seal of approval, continues to be as solid as ever, while 5...♘c6 is also reasonable for Black. The only real certainty is that White should prefer the Panov Attack to 4 dxc6, which would be a computer's choice, but is a miserable option for mere humans.

1 e4 d5 2 exd5 ♘f6 3 c4 c6

4 d4 *(D)*
    4 dxc6 - *game 70*
4...cxd5 5 ♘c3 ♘c6 *(D)*
    5...e6 6 ♘f3 *(D)*
        6...♗e7 - *game 73*
        6...♗b4 - *game 74*
    5...g6 - *game 75*

6 ♘f3 - *game 71*
6 ♗g5 - *game 72*

    4 d4   *5...♘c6*   *6 ♘f3*

CHAPTER ELEVEN

2...♘f6: Icelandic Gambit

1 e4 d5 2 exd5 ♘f6 3 c4 e6

The imaginative Icelandic Gambit came to prominence in the late 1980s, when young Icelandic International Masters such as Hannes Stefansson and Throstur Thorhallsson utilised it with some success. Black's concept is quite simple: a pawn is sacrificed in order to open lines and to develop quickly and effectively. Black will often castle long, park the rooks in the centre and then try to create annoying threats as soon as possible. It is important for Black to do this, because if White consolidates, Black can just wind up a clear pawn down. Frequently Black must be prepared to sacrifice further material in the quest to hunt down the white king while it remains in the centre. Needless to say, White has to tread very carefully throughout the opening stages in order to emerge unscathed.

From a theoretical standpoint White should be able to keep an advantage. Somehow, the Icelandic Gambit just looks as though it should not quite work for Black. Nevertheless, Black's practical results have been good and the gambit still carries that surprise punch.

Game 76
Dolmatov-Boissonet
Buenos Aires 1991

1 e4 d5 2 exd5 ♘f6 3 c4 e6

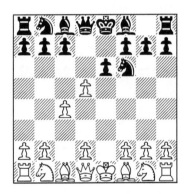

4 dxe6

The unambitious 4 d4?! exd5 5 ♘c3 ♗b4! just hands Black a good version of the Exchange French. Black can develop freely and has no problems whatsoever.

4...♗xe6 5 ♘f3

For 5 d4 see Games 79-82.

5...♘c6

The most natural move. The tricky alternative 5...♕e7!? is discussed in Game 78.

6 d4

The less testing 6 ♗e2 is seen in the next game.

6...♗b4+

Black must develop swiftly in order to create concrete threats, since White's position has no real weaknesses. Icelandic GM Hannes Stefansson, an expert on this line, has also tried 6...♕e7, albeit in a rapidplay game. Oll-Stefansson, Oviedo 1993, continued 7 ♗e3 0-0-0 8 ♘bd2 ♗f5 9 ♗e2 ♘b4 10 ♖c1 ♘xa2 and Stefansson had managed to win the pawn back, but only at the cost of giving White a ready-made attack on the a-file.

7 ♘c3 ♘e4 8 ♗d2 ♘xd2 9 ♕xd2 ♕e7 10 0-0-0

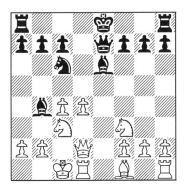

10...0-0

After this move Black's counterplay seems to fizzle out. Stefansson tested 10...0-0-0 against Michael Hennigan at Oakham 1988, but after 11 a3 ♗c5 12 d5 ♗g4 13 ♖e1 ♕f8 14 b4! ♗xf3 15 bxc5 ♗h5 16 ♕e3! ♘a5 17 ♕h3+ ♔b8 18 ♕xh5 ♕xc5 19 ♕e2 Hennigan was a piece to the good. Stefansson did go on to win the game, but at this point Black had insufficient play for the knight.

11 a3 ♘a5 12 ♔b1 ♗f5+ 13 ♔a2 ♗xc3 14 ♕xc3 b6 15 ♗d3

White has consolidated in an efficient manner and is now just a clear central pawn up.

15...♕f6 16 ♖he1 ♖fe8 17 h3 h6 18 ♗xf5 ♕xf5 19 d5!

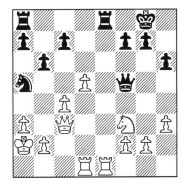

Putting the spare pawn to good use. Black soon gets overwhelmed in the centre and on the kingside.

19...♘b7 20 g4 ♕d7 21 ♘e5 ♕d6 22 h4 ♕f6 23 ♕g3 ♘d6 24 f4 g6 25 g5! ♕f5 26 ♘g4! ♖xe1 27 ♘xh6+ ♔f8 28 ♘xf5 ♖xd1 29 ♘xd6 cxd6 30 f5!

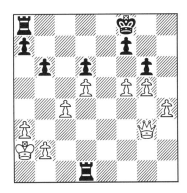

Black's position has just collapsed.

30...gxf5 31 ♕xd6+ ♔g8 32 h5 1-0

There is no satisfactory defence to

豐f6 followed by h5-h6. A faultless performance by Dolmatov. Is this the refutation of the Icelandic Gambit?

1 e4 d5 2 exd5 ⁅f6 3 c4 e6 4 dxe6 ⁅xe6 5 ⁅f3 ⁅c6 6 ⁅e2

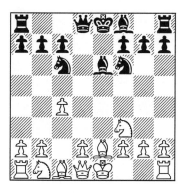

Voluntarily conceding the d4-square, in order to concentrate on development.

6...⁅c5 7 0-0 豐d7

This is probably the most flexible choice. Black plans a rapid ...0-0-0, applying pressure on White's backward d-pawn and the weak d4-square. Occupying that outpost at once has its drawbacks: after 7...⁅d4 8 ⁅xd4 豐xd4 9 d3 0-0-0 10 ⁅d2! ⁅d6 11 ⁅f3 豐b6 12 d4! White had achieved his aim of advancing the d-pawn and hence stood clearly better in Adams-Thorhallsson, Arnhem 1988.

8 a3

This move prepares the lunge b2-b4. The immediate 8 b4, offering a pawn sacrifice, was tried in the game Bibby-P.H.Nielsen, London (Lloyds

Bank) 1990. Nielsen declined the offer with 8...⁅d4, and after 9 ⁅c3 0-0-0 10 ⁅b2 ⁅xb4 11 ⁅xd4 豐xd4 12 豐a4 ⁅c6 an unclear position had been reached. White has some attacking chances on the queenside, but Black is still well centralised and has some active pieces. Grabbing the pawn with 8...⁅xb4 also does not look bad. IM Andrew Martin suggests 9 d4 ⁅g4 10 ⁅b2 0-0-0 11 d5 ⁅a5! with counterplay.

8...0-0-0 9 ⁅c3 ⁅he8 10 b4 ⁅d4

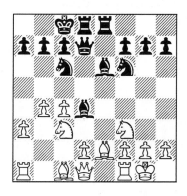

So White has succeeded in gaining some space on the queenside with a2-a3 and b2-b4, but meanwhile Black has centralised his pieces and they are now ready to occupy menacing posts. Psychologically this is a very difficult position for White, who is a pawn up but in effect 'playing Black'.

11 ⁅b2 ⁅g4 12 ⁅b1 ⁅f5 13 ⁅c1 ⁅e4 14 b5

Or 14 ⁅xe4 ⁅xb2 15 ⁅c5 豐d6 and Black picks up the exchange, as the white rook has no squares.

14...⁅e5 15 ⁅xe5 ⁅xe5 16 d3

Black was threatening 16...⁅xd2 17 豐xd2 ⁅xf2+, but 16 d3 allows another powerful combination.

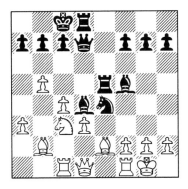

16...♘xf2! 17 ♖xf2 ♗xf2+ 18 ♔xf2 ♕d4+ 19 ♔f1 ♖xe2! 20 ♘xe2

Forced, as 20 ♔xe2 ♗g4+ and 20 ♕xe2 ♗xd3 both drop the queen. The upshot of all these tactics is that Black wins the pawn back, while the white pieces remain totally uncoordinated.

20...♕xb2 21 ♖c3 ♗g4 22 ♖c2 ♕xa3 23 ♖d2 ♕c5 24 h3 ♖d6!

The net begins to envelop the white king. 25 hxg4 ♖f6+ leads to mate.

25 d4 ♖f6+ 26 ♔g1 ♕e7 27 ♕e1

Or 27 hxg4 ♕e3+ 28 ♔h2 ♖h6 mate.

27...♕e3+ 28 ♔h2 ♗xh3! 0-1

29 gxh3 ♖f2+ 30 ♔h1 (30 ♔g1 ♖xe2+) 30...♕f3+ (or 30...♕xh3+) 31

♔g1 ♕g2 is mate. A skilful demonstration of Black's attacking chances in the Icelandic Gambit.

Game 78
Ageichenko-Maliutin
Moscow Open 1991

---

1 e4 d5 2 exd5 ♘f6 3 c4 e6 4 dxe6 ♗xe6 5 ♘f3 ♕e7!?

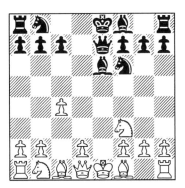

With the unsubtle threat of a discovered check, which is actually quite difficult to meet.

6 ♗e2

Returning the material, in the hope of later exploiting Black's queen on the e-file. Another critical move must be 6 ♕e2, which blocks in the f1-bishop but does retain the extra pawn. The game Grabics-Carvalho, Bratislava (World Under-18 Championship) 1993, continued 6...♘c6 7 d4 ♗f5 8 d5 ♘b4 9 ♕xe7+ ♗xe7 10 ♘a3 0-0-0 11 ♘d4 ♗g6 12 ♗e2 c6! 13 ♗f4 ♖he8 14 0-0 ♗c5 15 ♘b3 ♖xe2 16 ♘xc5 cxd5 17 ♘b5 ♘c6 18 ♘d6+ ♖xd6 19 ♗xd6 dxc4 20 ♖ac1 ♖xb2 21 ♖xc4 ♖xa2 with an unclear position, although there may well have been some improvements for both colours down the line.

6...♗xc4 7 ♘c3?!

I don't like this move, as it allows Black to simplify into an extremely comfortable position. Much more testing is 7 d3!, putting the question to the bishop. After 7...♗a6 8 0-0 ♕d8 9 d4 ♗e7 10 ♗xa6 ♘xa6 11 ♘c3 c6 12 ♖e1 0-0 13 ♕b3 ♖b8 14 ♗f4 ♗d6 15 ♗g5 White had kept an edge in Kuczynski-Damaso, Debrecen 1992. 7...♗e6, intending ...g7-g6 and ...♗g7 may be an improvement for Black.

7...♗xe2 8 ♘xe2 g6 9 ♕b3 c6 10 d4 ♕b4+! 11 ♕xb4 ♗xb4+ 12 ♗d2 ♘a6 13 ♗xb4 ♘xb4

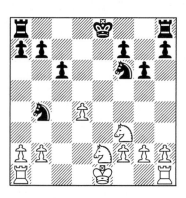

The exchange of queens increases the importance of White's weak d-pawn.

14 0-0 0-0-0 15 ♘c3 ♖he8 16 ♖fe1 ♘d3 17 ♖xe8 ♖xe8 18 b3 ♘e4 19 ♘xe4 ♖xe4 20 ♔f1 f6 21 a3 ♘f4 22 ♖e1 ♖xe1+ 23 ♘xe1 ♔d7 24 g3 ♘e6 25 ♘c2 c5!

It is somewhat surprising to liquidate White's only weakness, but this move proves to be very effective, as Black's king becomes dominant.

26 dxc5 ♘xc5 27 b4 ♘e4 28 ♔e2 ♔c6

Intending the simple ...♔c6-b5-a4 manoeuvre. White feels obliged to prevent this, but in doing so the advanced queenside pawns become 'sitting ducks'.

29 f3 ♘d6 30 a4 ♘c4 31 ♘d4+ ♔d5 32 ♘b5 a6 33 ♘c7+ ♔d4

Finally the black king penetrates. White's queenside is doomed; the only chance lies in a desperate counterattack on the other wing.

34 ♘e8 f5 35 ♘f6 ♔c3 36 b5?

36 ♘xh7 ♔xb4 37 ♘f8 was White's last throw of the dice.

36...a5! 37 ♘xh7 ♔b4 38 ♘f8 ♔xa4 39 ♘xg6 ♔b3 40 ♘f4 a4

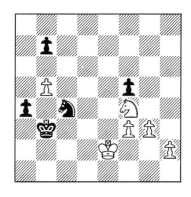

Knights are notoriously feeble when stopping rook's pawns and this is no exception.

41 ♔d1 a3 42 ♘d3 ♘b2+ 0-1

Game 79
Ioseliani-Gurieli
Tbilisi 1987

---

1 e4 d5 2 exd5 ♘f6 3 c4 e6 4 dxe6 ♗xe6 5 d4

5 d4 is a significant alternative to 5 ♘f3. Nevertheless, it does present Black with more attacking options.

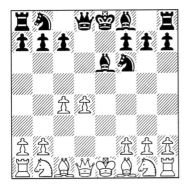

5...♗b4+ 6 ♗d2

Game 82 deals with 6 ♘c3.

6...♕e7

The alternative is 6....♗xd2+, as in Game 81.

7 ♗e2

7 ♗xb4 is the subject of the next game.

7...♘c6!

The tempting 7...♗xc4 falls short after 8 ♕a4+ ♘c6 9 ♗xb4 ♕xb4+ 10 ♕xb4 ♘xb4 11 ♗xc4 ♘c2+ 12 ♔d2 ♘xa1 13 ♘c3 0-0-0 14 ♘f3, when White will pick up the knight on a1 with a distinct advantage. With 7...♘c6 Black offers a piece sacrifice which is quite characteristic of the Icelandic Gambit.

8 d5 ♘xd5 9 cxd5 ♗xd5 10 ♔f1 0-0-0 11 ♕e1 ♗xd2 12 ♘xd2 ♔b8 13 ♗f3 ♕d6! 14 ♗xd5 ♕xd5 15 ♘gf3 ♖he8 16 ♕c1 ♕d3+ 17 ♔g1 ♖e2

see following diagram

An important moment. Black has obtained only one pawn for the piece, but White has still some way to go before consolidation is complete.

18 ♕c4

In her notes to the game Gurieli also gives the line 18 ♕c3!? ♘e5! 19 ♕xd3 (or 19 ♘xe5?! ♕xc3 20 bxc3 ♖dxd2 as 21 ♘g4 runs into 21...f5!) 19...♘xd3 20 ♖f1 ♘xb2, and Black has excellent compensation for the piece. With 18 ♕c4, White opts to return some of the excess material in the hope of simplifying the position.

18...♖xd2 19 ♘xd2 ♕xd2 20 ♕c3 ♕e2!?

Trading queens may have been the best bet here: 20...♕xc3!? 21 bxc3 ♖d3 22 g3 ♖xc3 23 ♔g2 a5 gives a roughly level ending.

21 h4 ♖d2 22 ♖f1 ♘d4 23 ♖h3??

The first instalment of a double blunder. 23 ♕e3! leaves White with an edge.

23...c5??

The simple 23...♖d1! 24 ♖xd1 ♕xd1+ 25 ♔h2 ♘e2 would have forced resignation, as 26 ♖d3 ♕g1+ 27 ♔h3 ♕h1+ 28 ♔g4 ♕xg2+ 29 ♖g3 ♕e4+ will be followed by 30...♘xc3.

24 ♖e3!

An excellent recovery! Now Black is forced into an inferior endgame where White's rooks will cause havoc.

24...♖c2 25 ♕a5 b6 26 ♕a4 ♕b5 27 ♕xb5 ♘xb5 28 ♖e7! ♖xb2 29 ♖xf7 ♘c7 30 ♖d1! ♖xa2

This move relinquishes the knight, but it is difficult to suggest a better alternative for Black here.

31 ♖d8+ ♔b7 32 ♖dd7 b5 33 ♖xc7+ ♔b6 34 ♖b7+ ♔c6 35 ♖fc7+ ♔d6 36 ♖xa7 ♖c2 37 ♖xg7 ♔d5 38 ♖g4 h5 39 ♖g5+ ♔c4 40 ♖xc5+ 1-0

40... ♔xc5 allows 41 ♖c7+ and 42 ♖xc2. A White win, but even so Black can be satisfied with the outcome of the opening.

Game 80
Kuijf-Hodgson
Wijk aan Zee 1989

---

1 e4 d5 2 exd5 ♘f6 3 c4 e6 4 dxe6 ♗xe6 5 d4 ♗b4+ 6 ♗d2 ♕e7 7 ♗xb4 ♕xb4+

---

see following diagram

---

8 ♕d2

After 8 ♘d2 Black should reply with the fearless 8...♘c6!, with two possible variations:

a) 9 d5 0-0-0! 10 dxc6 (10 dxe6 ♖he8 11 ♗e2 ♖xe6 gives Black an irresistible attack, while 10 ♘f3 transposes to

[b] below) 10...♖he8 11 ♗e2 ♘e4 and Black's compensation is quite obvious.

b) 9 ♘gf3 0-0-0 10 d5 ♗g4 11 ♗e2 ♗xf3 12 ♗xf3 ♖he8+ 13 ♔f1 ♘d4 14 ♕c1 ♘xf3 15 ♘xf3 ♖e4 16 b3 ♖de8 17 h3 ♘h5! 18 g3 ♘xg3+! 19 fxg3 ♖e3 20 ♘g1 ♕d6 21 ♖h2 ♖xg3 22 ♕b2 ♕g6 23 ♔f2 ♖ee3 24 ♘e2 ♖gf3+ 25 ♔e1 ♕g1+ 26 ♔d2 ♕xh2 27 ♖e1 ♕f2 and White resigned in A.Sokolov-Speelman, Madrid 1988. This is the game which catapulted the Icelandic Gambit into the limelight.

8...♘c6 9 ♘c3 0-0-0 10 d5 ♗g4 11 f3 ♖he8+ 12 ♗e2 ♗f5 13 0-0-0 ♘a5 14 g4

14...♗g6 15 ♘h3?

15 b3 is more resolute, although I still prefer Black after 15...c6!

15...♘d7 16 ♘b1?

And here 16 ♗d3!? was White's last hope. 16 ♘b1 allows a pretty combination.

16...♕b3!!

Very visual, as well as being extremely effective. Now 17 axb3 fails to 17...♘b3 mate, so the critical a-pawn drops.

17 ♗d3 ♕xa2 18 ♕b4 ♖e2!

White's bishop on d3 is overloaded, so he must give up the queen.

19 ♗xe2 ♘b3+ 20 ♕xb3 ♕xb3 21 ♖d2 ♕e3 0-1

An exceptional game from Julian Hodgson. It seems that Black has substantial hacking chances after the capture 7 ♗xb4.

> ### Game 81
> **Prill-Gurieli**
> *Badenweiler Open 1990*

1 e4 d5 2 exd5 ♘f6 3 c4 e6 4 dxe6 ♗xe6 5 d4 ♗b4+ 6 ♗d2 ♗xd2+

Another perfectly acceptable move, which may be even stronger than 6...♕e7. In any case 6...♗xd2+ pres-

ents White with just as many problems.

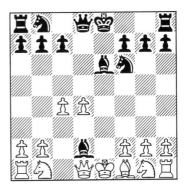

7 ♕xd2 ♕e7 8 ♕e2?!

After this move White is really struggling to stay afloat. 8 ♕e3 is stronger, although after analysing it I believe that White still has to walk a very long and thin tightrope. Following 8...♘c6! we have:

a) 9 d5? ♘g4! 10 ♕c3 ♗xd5+ 11 ♘e2 ♗e6 12 ♕xg7 0-0-0 and Black's lead in development is utterly overwhelming.

b) 9 ♘f3 0-0-0 and now:

b1) 10 d5? ♖he8! 11 dxe6 (or 11 dxc6 ♘g4! 12 cxb7+ ♔b8 and White is helpless against the assortment of devastating threats) 11...♘g4 12 ♕e2 ♕b4+ and Black wins.

b2) 10 ♗e2!? ♖he8 11 d5 (11 0-0 ♗g4! 12 ♘c3 ♗xf3 13 ♗xf3 ♕b4 14 ♕g5 ♘xd4 was good for Black in Romilly-And.Martin, Aberdeen 1991) 11...♘b4!? 12 0-0! (12 ♘d4 c5! 13 dxc6 ♖xd4! wins) 12...♗xd5!? (12...♘c2 13 ♕xa7 is also unclear) 13 cxd5 ♕xe3 14 fxe3 ♘c2 15 ♘c3 ♘xa1 16 ♖xa1 ♘xd5 17 ♘xd5 ♖xd5. Finally the smoke has cleared, leaving a roughly level endgame.

8...②c6 9 ②f3 0-0-0

10 ②bd2

Tamely surrendering the extra pawn, but 10 d5 ☐he8! is the same old story: 11 ②c3 ♗xd5! 12 cxd5 ♕b4 13 dxc6 ♕xb2!, 11 dxe6 ♕b4+ and 11 dxc6 ♗xc4 are all winning for Black.

10...②xd4 11 ②xd4 ☐xd4 12 ☐d1 ☐e8 13 g3 ♗g4!

This move is a killer. White is forced to give up the queen.

14 f3 ♕b4 15 ♕xe8+ ②xe8 16 fxg4 ②f6 17 ☐g1 ♕e7+ 18 ♗e2 ②xg4 19 ☐c1 ♕e3 0-1

So Black has good counterchances after 5 d4 ♗b4+ 6 ♗d2. In the next game we see why 6 ②c3 is considered to be even worse.

Game 82
Thirion-Berend
Eupen 1995

1 e4 d5 2 exd5 ②f6 3 c4 e6 4 dxe6 ♗xe6 5 d4 ♗b4+ 6 ②c3

Not to be recommended!

6...②e4! 7 ♕d3

7 a3 ②xc3 8 ♕d3 has been suggested, but after 8...♕e7! 9 axb4 ♗xc4+ 10 ♕e3 ♗xf1 11 ♕xe7+ ♚xe7 12 ♚xf1 ②d5 White has only obtained a miserable endgame.

7...♗f5 8 ♕e3

8 ♕f3 is refuted by 8...♗xd4! 9 ②ge2 ♕d7 10 a3 ②c6 11 ♗f4 ②e5 12 ♕e3 ②d3+ 13 ♚d1 ♗c5 0-1 Ruxton-Hsu, Tunja 1989. Perhaps 8 ②ge2 is relatively best, although 8...②xc3! 9 ♕xf5 ②b5+ 10 ♗d2 ♗xd2+ 11 ♚xd2 ②xd4 still looks good for Black.

8...0-0 9 ②ge2 ☐e8 10 ♕f3 ②xc3 11 bxc3 ♕xd4!

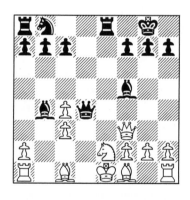

Cleverly exploiting all the pins. White is already busted.

12 ♗d2 ♕e5 13 ♕e3 ♗c5 14 ♕xe5 ☐xe5 15 ♗f4 ☐e7 16 0-0-0 ♗a3+ 17 ♚d2 ②a6 18 ②d4 ☐d8 19 ☐e1 ☐xd4+! 0-1

Summary

Despite a number of wins in this chapter, Black still requires an improvement over the Dolmatov-Boissonet game, which looks extremely convincing from White's point of view. Perhaps we will see more of 5...♕e7!? as an answer to 5 ♞f3. In any case, it is clear that this move remains Black's only real problem, as after 5 d4 ♝b4+ 6 ♝d2, both 6...♕e7 and 6...♝xd2+ look perfectly satisfactory.

1 e4 d5 2 exd5 ♞f6 3 c4 e6

4 dxe6 ♝xe6 5 ♞f3 *(D)*
    5 d4 ♝b4+
        6 ♝d2
            6...♕e7 *(D)*
                7 ♝e2 - *game 79*
                7 ♝xb4 - *game 80*
            6...♝xd2+ - *game 81*
        6 ♞c3 - *game 82*
5...♞c6 *(D)*
    5...♕e7 - *game 78*
6 d4 - *game 76*
6 ♝e2 - *game 77*

5 ♞f3

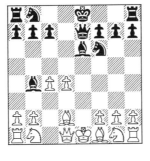

6...♕e7

5...♞c6

INDEX OF COMPLETE GAMES